PYTHON IN ECONOMETRICS

Hayden Vander Post

Reactive Publishing

To my daughter, may she know anything is possible.

CONTENTS

INTRODUCTION

Welcome to the exciting world of "Python in Econometrics: Bridging Data Science and Economic Analysis." In this book, we embark on a journey that will equip you with the skills and knowledge to leverage the power of Python for econometric analysis, predictive modeling, and data-driven decision-making.

Have you ever wondered how economists forecast economic trends, assess policy impacts, or unravel the intricacies of financial markets? Or perhaps you've pondered the magic behind data-driven decision-making, which fuels industries and governments alike. If you're intrigued by these questions, then you're about to embark on a thrilling exploration that will unlock the answers.

Economics, the study of how societies allocate resources, and Python, the versatile programming language, may appear to have little in common at first glance. However, when combined, they form a formidable duo that can tackle complex economic problems, unveil hidden insights in data, and drive impactful policy decisions.

Consider this: With Python, you can effortlessly clean, explore, and visualize economic data, then apply advanced econometric techniques to derive meaningful insights. You can predict future economic trends, model the impact of policy changes, and even build simulations to test hypotheses.

In this book, you'll learn how to harness the capabilities of Python to:

Master the fundamentals of econometrics.

Seamlessly integrate data science into economic analysis.

Dive into time series analysis, panel data modeling, and more.

Apply machine learning to economic predictions.

Create striking data visualizations that enhance your ability to communicate complex economic insights.

Are you excited yet? You should be, because this journey is not just about acquiring skills; it's about unveiling the true potential of economic analysis in the digital age. Whether you're an economist, a data scientist, a policy analyst, or a student eager to learn, this book is designed to empower you with the tools and techniques needed to excel in your field.

As we progress through these chapters, you'll not only build a strong foundation in Python and econometrics but also apply your knowledge to real-world economic problems. Each chapter contains practical examples, hands-on exercises, and case studies that illustrate the principles and techniques covered. By the end of this journey, you'll have the skills to tackle complex economic questions with confidence and precision.

So, let's embark on this exciting voyage, where Python and econometrics converge to uncover the hidden patterns in economic data, provide deeper insights into economic phenomena, and empower you to make data-driven decisions. It's time to unlock the full potential of Python in econometrics and transform the way you approach economic analysis. Let's begin!

CHAPTER 1: INTRODUCTION TO PYTHON AND ECONOMETRICS

Why Python in Econometrics?

Welcome to the first section of this journey into the world of Python in econometrics. In this chapter, we'll explore why Python is a powerful tool for economists and econometricians. Python, with its versatility and rich libraries, offers a multitude of advantages that make it an ideal choice for econometric analysis.

Python is renowned for its simplicity and readability, making it a great language for beginners and experienced programmers alike. In the realm of econometrics, this simplicity translates into an accessible tool for those who want to harness the power of data science and economic analysis.

Versatility and Rich Libraries

One of the key reasons economists turn to Python is its versatility. It's not just a programming language; it's a complete ecosystem for data analysis and modeling. Here are some compelling advantages:

Pandas for Data Handling: Python's Pandas library allows for efficient data manipulation and analysis. With Pandas, you can easily load, clean, and transform data, essential for econometric work.

python

```python
import pandas as pd

# Load data from a CSV file
data = pd.read_csv('economic_data.csv')

# Clean the data
data.dropna(inplace=True)

# Calculate summary statistics
mean = data.mean()
```

NumPy for Numerical Computing: NumPy is the backbone for numerical operations in Python. It provides support for large, multi-dimensional arrays and matrices. In econometrics, this is crucial for matrix algebra.

python

```python
import numpy as np

# Create a NumPy array
x = np.array()

# Perform matrix operations
```

```python
result = np.dot(x, x)
```

Matplotlib for Data Visualization: Visualization is a powerful tool in economic analysis. Matplotlib offers a wide range of plotting options to convey your findings effectively.

python

```python
import matplotlib.pyplot as plt

# Create a line plot
plt.plot(data, data)
plt.xlabel('Year')
plt.ylabel('GDP')
plt.title('GDP Over Time')
plt.show()
```

Scikit-Learn for Machine Learning: Machine learning is increasingly valuable in economics. Scikit-Learn provides a comprehensive toolkit for regression, classification, clustering, and more.

python

```python
from sklearn.linear_model import LinearRegression

# Create a linear regression model
model = LinearRegression()

# Fit the model to your data
model.fit(X, y)
```

Predict economic trends

predictions = model.predict(new_data)

Jupyter Notebooks for Interactive Analysis: Jupyter Notebooks allow you to create and share documents that combine live code, equations, visualizations, and narrative text. It's an ideal platform for documenting and presenting econometric analyses.

Python's rich libraries continue to grow, making it a dynamic and evolving environment for econometricians. From machine learning to deep learning, Python has it all.

Python is a favorite among economists because it's open-source and has a thriving community. This means that you're never alone in your journey. You can seek help, share your findings, and collaborate with experts from various fields.

As we delve deeper into this book, you'll discover how Python's versatility and rich libraries can be harnessed for specific econometric tasks. From basic regression analysis to advanced machine learning and economic modeling, Python has the tools you need.

Are you ready to embark on this exciting journey of learning Python for econometrics? Let's continue our exploration, as we move on to setting up your Python environment in the next section.

Setting Up Your Python Environment

Now that we've explored the enticing reasons behind using

Python in econometrics, it's time to roll up our sleeves and get started. In this section, we'll delve into the process of setting up your Python environment, a crucial step in your journey to mastering econometric analysis.

A Smooth Takeoff

Before we dive into coding and analysis, let's ensure that your Python environment is in tip-top shape. This is your virtual workspace, your laboratory, where you'll perform experiments with data and models. It's essential for this workspace to be well-organized and ready for action.

Choosing an Integrated Development Environment (IDE)

First, you'll need an Integrated Development Environment, commonly known as an IDE. Think of it as your command center for all things Python. An IDE is a software application that provides comprehensive facilities to programmers for software development.

There are several IDEs available, each with its own set of features and advantages. One of the most popular choices among Python enthusiasts is Jupyter Notebook. It offers a web-based interactive computing environment ideal for data science and analysis.

To set up Jupyter Notebook, you can use Python's package manager, pip, to install it. Open your command prompt or terminal and type:

python

```
pip install jupyter
```

Once the installation is complete, you can launch Jupyter Notebook by running the following command:

```
python
```

```
jupyter notebook
```

The Jupyter Notebook interface will open in your web browser, allowing you to create and run Python code cells.

Virtual Environments for Isolation

Python has a remarkable capability to allow you to create isolated environments. These are like separate compartments for your Python projects, each with its own set of dependencies. Why is this important? It's to ensure that changes you make for one project don't inadvertently affect another.

To create a virtual environment, you can use the built-in venv module. Navigate to your project directory and run:

```
python
```

```
python -m venv myenv
```

This command creates a virtual environment named 'myenv' in your project folder. You can activate it by using:

On Windows:

```
python
```

```
myenv\Scripts\activate
```

On macOS and Linux:

```
python
```

```
source myenv/bin/activate
```

You'll notice that your command prompt or terminal now indicates the activated environment. Anything you install using pip while the environment is active will be specific to that environment.

Managing Dependencies with Pip

Python's package manager, pip, is your trusted ally when it comes to managing dependencies. You can use it to install libraries, frameworks, and packages. For example, to install the Pandas library, you can simply run:

```
python
```

```
pip install pandas
```

This will fetch and install the Pandas library, making it available for use in your Python projects.

Version Control with Git

For any serious coding endeavor, especially one that involves collaboration or ongoing development, it's essential to use version control. Git, a distributed version control system, is widely adopted in the programming community.

To get started with Git, download and install it from the official website (https://git-scm.com/). Once installed, open your command prompt or terminal and configure your name and email address:

python

git config --global .name "Your Name"
git config --global .email "youremail@example.com"

With Git, you can track changes in your code, collaborate with others seamlessly, and maintain a history of your project's development.

Next Steps

With your Python environment set up, you're now ready to embark on your econometric journey. In the following chapters, we'll introduce you to essential Python concepts, cover the fundamentals of econometrics, and guide you through creating your first Python program in the context of econometric analysis.

Remember, your Python environment is your workbench, and like any good craftsman, you want it to be well-organized and equipped with the best tools. The choices you've made today will make your journey into the world of Python in econometrics an efficient and enjoyable one. So, let's keep the engines running, as we move forward to the next chapter, where we'll dive into the very essence of Python – its basic concepts.

Basic Python Concepts

As we venture further into the realm of Python in econometrics, it's essential to establish a solid foundation in the language. In this section, we'll delve into the fundamental building blocks of Python – its data types, variables, and control structures. These are the very elements that will empower you to harness the true potential of this versatile language.

The ABCs of Data Types

Python, like a versatile toolbox, offers a variety of data types that allow you to handle different kinds of information. Think of data types as containers, each designed to hold specific types of data, be it numbers, text, or even complex structures. Let's explore some of the fundamental data types in Python:

Integers (int): These are whole numbers. For example, 1, 42, and -10 are all integers. In Python, you can perform arithmetic operations with integers, making it a valuable data type for mathematical operations.

Floats (float): Floats, or floating-point numbers, represent real numbers and can include decimal points. Examples include 3.14 and -0.01. Floats are crucial when dealing with measurements, scientific data, and more.

Strings (str): Strings are sequences of characters, which can include letters, numbers, and special symbols. For example, "Hello, Python!" and 'Econometrics123' are strings. Python provides a rich set of operations for working with strings, including concatenation and slicing.

Booleans (bool): Booleans have only two possible values: True and False. They are essential in controlling the flow of your programs and making decisions. For instance, you can use booleans to create conditions, like if x > 5, to execute specific code.

Lists (list): Lists are versatile data structures that can hold a collection of values, whether they're integers, floats, strings, or even other lists. For instance, my_list = is a list containing a mix of data types.

Dictionaries (dict): Dictionaries are like lookup tables with key-value pairs. They allow you to store and retrieve data based on a unique key. For example, student = {'name': 'John', 'age': 20, 'major': 'Economics'} is a dictionary.

Tuples (tuple): Tuples are similar to lists, but with one crucial difference: they are immutable. Once you create a tuple, you cannot change its elements. This can be useful when you want to ensure data integrity.

Variables: Your Data's Home

In Python, variables act as containers for storing and managing data. Think of them as labeled boxes that hold values of different data types. You can give a variable any name you like, provided you follow certain naming rules:

Variable names are case-sensitive, so my_var and My_Var are different.

Variable names must start with a letter (a-z, A-Z) or an underscore (_).

They can be followed by letters, numbers, or underscores.

Here's a simple example of creating and using variables:

python

```
x = 5  # Assigning an integer value to a variable x
name = 'Alice'  # Assigning a string value to a variable name
is_student = True  # Assigning a boolean value to a variable is_student
```

Variables are the glue that holds your Python programs together. They allow you to store, retrieve, and manipulate data dynamically.

Control Structures: Directing the Flow

Control structures are like the steering wheel of your Python programs, helping you navigate the flow of execution. There are three primary control structures to master:

Conditional Statements (if, else, elif): Conditional statements are your way of making decisions in Python. You can check conditions and execute different code blocks based on whether those conditions are met. For instance:

python

```
x = 10
if x > 5:
```

```python
    print("x is greater than 5")
else:
    print("x is not greater than 5")
```

Loops (for and while): Loops allow you to repeat a set of instructions multiple times. A for loop iterates over a sequence (e.g., a list), while a while loop repeats until a specific condition becomes False.

python

```python
# Example of a for loop
fruits =
for fruit in fruits:
    print(fruit)

# Example of a while loop
count = 0
while count < 5:
    print(count)
    count += 1
```

Functions: Functions are like reusable blocks of code that you can call by name. They allow you to encapsulate specific tasks and parameters. Functions make your code modular and easier to maintain.

python

```python
def greet(name):
```

```
print(f"Hello, {name}!")
```

```
greet("Alice")
```

The Journey Continues

Armed with these foundational Python concepts, you're now equipped to begin your voyage into the fascinating world of econometric analysis. As you proceed, you'll find that these data types, variables, and control structures form the backbone of your Python programs. They enable you to manipulate and analyze economic data with precision, opening up a world of possibilities in the realm of economics. In the next chapter, we'll explore the intriguing field of econometrics, diving deeper into its key concepts and terminology. Stay curious, and let's embark on this exciting journey together.

Introduction to Econometrics

Econometrics is the beating heart of economics. It's where data science and economic analysis come together to unlock the intricate relationships that drive our world. But what is econometrics? Why is it so crucial for economists, and how does it fit into the grand scheme of Python?

Defining Econometrics

Econometrics, put simply, is the bridge that connects economic theory with real-world data. It's the science of using statistical and mathematical models to analyze and quantify economic relationships. As economists, we explore how different variables interact and influence each other in the complex economic landscape. Econometrics equips us with the tools to test economic theories rigorously, providing empirical evidence to support or refute our hypotheses.

Econometrics is an interdisciplinary field that borrows concepts from economics, mathematics, and statistics. Its primary goal is to transform data into actionable insights, allowing us to make informed decisions and policy recommendations.

Key Concepts and Terminology

Before we delve deeper into the world of econometrics, let's familiarize ourselves with some fundamental concepts and terminology that will accompany us throughout this book:

1. Dependent and Independent Variables: In econometrics, we often work with variables. The dependent variable is what we want to explain or predict, while independent variables are those we believe influence the dependent variable. For example, when analyzing factors affecting household consumption, consumption expenditure might be the dependent variable, and independent variables could include income, prices, and demographic data.

2. Regression Analysis: This is one of the cornerstones of econometrics. It's a statistical technique used to model the relationship between a dependent variable and one or more independent variables. Simple linear regression, as we'll explore in Chapter 3, is the most basic form, while multiple linear regression extends to multiple independent variables.

3. Hypothesis Testing: Economists use hypothesis testing to determine whether the relationships we observe in data are statistically significant. We set up null and alternative hypotheses and use statistical tests to determine if the evidence

supports the alternative hypothesis.

4. OLS (Ordinary Least Squares): OLS is a method used to estimate the parameters of a linear regression model. It finds the best-fitting line by minimizing the sum of the squared differences between the observed and predicted values.

5. Endogeneity: This occurs when an independent variable is correlated with the error term in a regression model. It's a common concern in econometrics, and addressing endogeneity is crucial for valid results.

6. Multicollinearity: When two or more independent variables in a regression model are highly correlated, it can lead to multicollinearity issues. Detecting and dealing with multicollinearity is essential to ensure the reliability of your model.

7. Heteroscedasticity: Heteroscedasticity refers to the situation where the variance of the residuals in a regression model is not constant. Detecting and correcting heteroscedasticity is vital to maintain the reliability of your model's predictions.

8. Autocorrelation: In time series data, autocorrelation occurs when a variable is correlated with its past values. Identifying and addressing autocorrelation is vital in time series analysis.

9. R-squared: This is a measure of how well the independent variables explain the variation in the dependent variable. It's a valuable metric for assessing the goodness of fit of a regression model.

10. P-values: P-values indicate the probability of observing the results you have when the null hypothesis is true. Low p-values

suggest that the evidence supports the alternative hypothesis.

In this chapter and throughout the book, we'll delve into these concepts, demystifying them and showing you how to apply them using Python. We'll combine the power of programming with the depth of economic analysis, providing you with the skills and knowledge to tackle real-world economic questions.

Econometrics is not just about equations and numbers; it's about understanding the world through data. We'll equip you with the tools to navigate this rich and complex landscape, and Python will be your trusty companion on this journey. As you immerse yourself in the realm of Python and econometrics, remember that you're not just learning a new skill; you're joining a community of economists and data scientists who use these tools to shape policies, make informed decisions, and uncover the hidden patterns that drive economies.

Your First Python Program in Econometrics

Welcome to the practical realm of Python in econometrics! By now, you've explored why Python is a vital tool for economists, set up your Python environment, grasped basic Python concepts, and gained an understanding of econometrics. Now, it's time to take the plunge and create your very first Python program in the context of econometric analysis.

Why Python for Econometrics?

Before we embark on this journey, let's revisit why Python is the go-to choice for econometricians. Python's versatility knows no bounds. It's an all-in-one package, combining easy-to-read syntax with a vast library ecosystem. For economists, this translates into a one-stop-shop for data analysis, visualization, and econometric modeling. Python libraries such as NumPy, pandas, Matplotlib, and StatsModels will be your trusty companions throughout this adventure.

Now, let's delve into the essential components of your first Python program in econometrics.

Step 1: Setting The Stage

In the context of econometric analysis, your Python program will often begin with importing libraries. For instance, you might start by importing NumPy and pandas. These libraries are powerhouses for data manipulation. NumPy excels in numerical operations, while pandas shines in handling structured data.

python

```
import numpy as np
import pandas as pd
```

Step 2: Loading Your Data

Data is the lifeblood of econometrics. To perform any analysis, you need data. For this example, we'll load a sample dataset using pandas. Let's assume you have a CSV file named 'econ_data.csv' containing your economic variables.

python

```
# Load the data
data = pd.read_csv('econ_data.csv')
```

Step 3: Exploring Your Data

Before diving into the hardcore econometric analysis, it's essential to familiarize yourself with your dataset. You can use the following lines of code to view the first few rows of your data and obtain some basic statistics:

python

```
# Display the first few rows
print(data.head())
```

```
# Get summary statistics
print(data.describe())
```

Step 4: Data Visualization

Econometrics is not just about numbers; it's also about conveying your findings visually. Matplotlib, one of Python's most popular visualization libraries, makes this easy. Let's create a simple scatter plot of two variables from your dataset:

python

```
import matplotlib.pyplot as plt
```

```
# Scatter plot
plt.scatter(data, data)
plt.xlabel('GDP')
plt.ylabel('Unemployment')
plt.title('GDP vs. Unemployment')
plt.show()
```

Step 5: Basic Econometric Analysis

Now, the real fun begins. Let's say you want to perform a simple linear regression to understand the relationship between GDP and unemployment. StatsModels is a fantastic library for this purpose:

python

```
import statsmodels.api as sm

# Prepare the data
X = data
y = data
X = sm.add_constant(X) # Add an intercept

# Fit the model
model = sm.OLS(y, X).fit()

# Print the regression summary
print(model.summary())
```

Congratulations, you've conducted your first econometric analysis with Python! The regression summary provides essential insights into the relationship between GDP and unemployment, including coefficients, p-values, and goodness-of-fit statistics.

Step 6: Interpretation And Next Steps

With the results in hand, it's time to interpret your findings.

Do the coefficients make economic sense? Are they statistically significant? What are the policy implications?

This is just the beginning. As you progress through this book, you'll dive deeper into advanced econometric techniques, time series analysis, panel data, machine learning, and more. Python is your gateway to unlocking the intricate relationships in economics, and the possibilities are endless.

As we wrap up this initial program, remember that learning Python in econometrics is an iterative process. The more you practice, the more proficient you'll become. Take your time to understand the nuances of Python, experiment with different models, and don't hesitate to ask questions. The journey to mastering Python in econometrics is filled with exciting challenges and discoveries, and we're here to guide you every step of the way.

So, what's next? Get ready to dive deeper into the world of econometric analysis as we tackle more complex models and real-world applications. Stay curious, keep practicing, and let your passion for economics drive your Python journey.

Conclusion: Embracing the Power of Python in Econometrics

In the opening chapter of "Python in Econometrics: Bridging Data Science and Economic Analysis," you embarked on an exciting journey to discover the dynamic synergy between Python and econometrics. You've seen the unparalleled versatility of Python and its rich libraries that are essential tools in the hands of economists.

As you've set up your Python environment, explored basic

Python concepts, and laid the foundation for econometric understanding, you're now equipped with the fundamentals needed to venture into more complex and intriguing aspects of economic analysis.

Chapter 2 Awaits, Where We Delve Into The Critical Realm Of "Data Preparation." Here, You'll Learn How To Harness Python's Capabilities To Process And Manipulate Data Effectively, Preparing It For The Rigorous Analysis That Lies Ahead. So, If You're Ready To Dive Deeper Into The Heart Of Econometrics, Turn The Page And Let's Unlock The True Potential Of Python In Economic Analysis.

CHAPTER 2:
NAVIGATING DATA'S
UNTAMED WATERS

Welcome to Chapter 2 of "Python in Econometrics: Bridging Data Science and Economic Analysis." In the previous chapter, you laid the groundwork for your Python journey and gained insight into the world of econometrics. Now, it's time to embark on a new and exciting expedition through the realm of "Data Preparation."

Imagine data as the raw material of your analysis, the building blocks of your economic insights. In this chapter, we will learn to wield the power of Python to master this raw material and transform it into a refined, workable form.

We'll explore data types, structures, and the various techniques for loading, cleaning, and transforming data. You will become adept at visualizing data to gain insights and embark on a real-world data case study to put your skills into practice.

The economic landscape is vast and ever-changing, but with Python as your compass, you will navigate these untamed waters with confidence and precision. So, let's dive into Chapter 2 and prepare to transform data into economic wisdom. Your adventure continues, and the journey ahead promises to be both enlightening and rewarding.

Data Types and Data Structures

In our quest to master Python for econometrics, it is essential to understand the very building blocks of this versatile language - data types and structures. Think of these as the tools in your kit, the elements with which you construct your data-driven analysis.

Understanding Data Types

Imagine you have a toolbox filled with various types of tools, each designed for specific tasks. Python, too, has its arsenal of data types, each tailored for particular data-handling functions.

One of the fundamental data types is the integer, which deals with whole numbers. For instance, when analyzing the quantity of products sold or the number of customers, you'll often work with integers.

Another critical data type is the floating-point number, or simply, the float, which accommodates decimal numbers. In financial analysis, you might use floats to handle price changes, interest rates, or economic growth rates.

Strings are another essential data type. Think of these as the words, sentences, and paragraphs in your data world. Strings are used for text analysis, parsing, and data manipulation.

Python allows you to create a variety of data structures to organize and manage data efficiently. One such structure is the list. A list is like a collection of data held together in an ordered sequence. You can think of it as a shopping list, where items are listed in a particular order. Lists are incredibly versatile and can hold data of different types.

In the world of econometrics, dictionaries are your go-to when dealing with structured data. A dictionary is like a bilingual translation book, with keys representing words in one language and values representing translations in another. Dictionaries are ideal for storing data as key-value pairs, making them a vital tool for managing economic data.

But our data journey doesn't end there. The star of the show in data manipulation is the dataframe, a two-dimensional, tabular data structure, much like a spreadsheet. Dataframes allow you to work with rows and columns, making it a breeze to analyze economic data sets, conduct statistical analyses, and visualize trends.

Now, you might be wondering why understanding these data types and structures is crucial. The answer lies in the foundation of Python's flexibility. As an economist, you'll find yourself dealing with an array of data types in your daily work. Whether you're working with large datasets, stock prices, GDP figures, or consumer surveys, your ability to comprehend and manipulate data types and structures will determine the efficiency and accuracy of your analysis.

To illustrate the power of these data structures, let's dive into some practical examples:

python

Working with Data Types

```python
# Integers
units_sold = 100
customers_served = 1500

# Floating-Point Numbers
interest_rate = 0.05
inflation_rate = 0.02

# Strings
country = "United States"
currency = "US Dollar"

# Lists
daily_stock_prices =
monthly_sales =

# Dictionaries
economic_indicators = {
    "GDP": 21459852,
    "Unemployment Rate": 3.9,
    "Inflation Rate": 1.8
}

# Dataframes (using the pandas library, as we'll explore in later
chapters)
import pandas as pd

data = {
```

```
    "Year": ,
    "GDP":
}

df = pd.DataFrame(data)
```

In the chapters to come, you will become intimately familiar with how these data types and structures facilitate the tasks of data analysis, econometric modeling, and economic forecasting.

As we set sail on this journey into Python's data handling capabilities, remember that mastering data types and structures is akin to understanding the tools in your toolbox. Each has its purpose, and together, they enable you to construct insightful economic analyses with confidence.

Loading and Reading Data

In the world of data analysis and econometrics, access to data is like a compass guiding your journey towards valuable insights. Python, as your trusty vessel, offers you a variety of tools to navigate this vast ocean of information. Let's hoist the sail and embark on our exploration of loading and reading data, a vital skill for every economist diving into the world of Python.

The Need for Data Loading

Imagine you're a captain of a ship about to embark on a grand adventure. Your ship, Python in this case, is ready, and your crew, a skilled team of libraries including pandas, is eager. What's missing? The treasure map, which is your data. But before you can start the journey, you must load this map.

Python excels at handling various data formats. The pandas library, often referred to as the workhorse of data analysis in Python, is here to help you on this quest. Whether your data is in CSV, Excel, SQL, or any other format, pandas has got your back.

Setting the Sails: Loading Data with Pandas

To load data with pandas, you will primarily use the read_csv() function for CSV files, read_excel() for Excel files, and read_sql() for SQL databases. Let's dive into an example of loading a CSV file:

python

```
import pandas as pd

# Loading data from a CSV file
data = pd.read_csv('your_data_file.csv')
```

This one-liner reads the data from a CSV file and stores it in a pandas dataframe, which is like a structured table for your data. Dataframes are versatile and allow you to perform various data manipulations.

Plotting a Course: Understanding Data Sources

Before you load your data, you need to know where it's located. Is it stored locally on your computer, or is it hosted on the web? The method of loading data might differ depending on its source.

For local data, you'll use the file path, like in the previous example. For web-hosted data, you can use a URL to load the data directly. Here's an example of loading data from a URL:

python

```
# Loading data from a URL
url = 'https://example.com/your_data_file.csv'
data = pd.read_csv(url)
```

Remember to ensure that you have an active internet connection when loading data from the web.

Casting the Nets: Data Exploration

Once you've loaded your data, it's time to cast your nets and explore it. Pandas provides a plethora of functions to give you insights into your dataset. You can use commands like head(), tail(), and info() to get a quick overview of your data, examine the first or last rows, and understand its structure.

For example:

python

```
# Display the first 5 rows of your dataset
print(data.head())

# Display the last 5 rows of your dataset
print(data.tail())

# Get information about your dataset
```

```
print(data.info())
```

These commands will help you get a sense of the data's content and structure, a crucial step before you dive into your analysis.

Finding Hidden Treasures: Data Cleaning

In your journey through the sea of data, you might encounter rough waters—data that's messy, inconsistent, or contains missing values. Fear not, for Python and pandas offer techniques to clean and prepare your data.

Data cleaning involves dealing with missing values, handling outliers, and data imputation. Here's a glimpse of what's in store:

python

```python
# Handling missing values
data.dropna() # Drop rows with missing values
data.fillna(value) # Fill missing values with a specific value

# Dealing with outliers
z_scores = (data - data.mean()) / data.std() # Calculate z-scores
outliers = (z_scores > threshold) | (z_scores < -threshold) # Define outliers
cleaned_data = data # Remove outliers

# Data imputation
data.interpolate() # Interpolate missing data points
```

These tools and techniques are essential for ensuring the integrity of your data and preparing it for analysis.

Plotting a Map: Data Visualization

After successfully loading and cleaning your data, the next step is to create a map to visualize and understand it. Data visualization is an art in itself, and Python provides you with tools like Matplotlib and Seaborn to craft compelling visual narratives.

For example, using Matplotlib, you can create a line plot to visualize trends in your data:

python

```
import matplotlib.pyplot as plt

plt.plot(data, data)
plt.xlabel('Date')
plt.ylabel('Price')
plt.title('Price Trend Over Time')
plt.show()
```

In this example, we're visualizing the price trends over time. Visualization can uncover patterns, anomalies, and insights that may remain hidden in raw data.

**A Real-World Expedition: Data Case Study

Data Cleaning

In the realm of data science and econometric analysis, one of the most critical steps in the data preparation phase is data cleaning. This process involves a systematic approach to handle various data issues, such as missing data, outliers, and data imputation. In this section, we will delve into the art of data cleaning and equip you with the necessary skills to ensure that your datasets are ready for analysis.

Handling Missing Data

Missing data is a common issue in real-world datasets. It can occur for various reasons, from technical errors during data collection to participants choosing not to answer certain questions in surveys. Dealing with missing data is essential to ensure that your analysis is accurate and reliable.

Strategies for Handling Missing Data

Deletion: One straightforward approach is to delete rows or columns containing missing data. While this is a quick solution, it may result in a significant loss of information, especially if the missing data is not completely random.

Imputation: Imputation is the process of estimating or

replacing missing values with plausible substitutes. Common imputation techniques include mean imputation, median imputation, and regression imputation. The choice of imputation method depends on the nature of the data and the specific research context.

Advanced Techniques: For more advanced s, techniques like k-Nearest Neighbors (k-NN) imputation, multiple imputations, or deep learning-based imputations can be employed. These methods can provide more accurate estimates and preserve the dataset's integrity.

Addressing Outliers

Outliers are data points that deviate significantly from the rest of the data. They can distort statistical analyses and modeling, making it crucial to identify and address them. Outliers can occur due to measurement errors, data entry errors, or genuinely extreme observations.

Identifying Outliers

Visualization: Data visualization is a powerful tool for identifying outliers. Box plots, scatter plots, and histograms can help you spot data points that fall far outside the typical range.

Statistical Tests: Various statistical tests, like the Z-score or the modified Z-score, can be used to identify outliers based on their deviation from the mean.

Handling Outliers

Transformation: Sometimes, transforming the data using

mathematical functions (e.g., log transformation) can make the distribution more suitable for analysis, effectively reducing the impact of outliers.

Capping or Flooring: For some analyses, it may be appropriate to cap (set a maximum value) or floor (set a minimum value) outliers to mitigate their influence.

Exclusion: In certain situations, outliers may represent extreme but valid observations. You can choose to exclude or include them based on the research question and context.

Data Imputation

Data imputation is the process of estimating values for missing or incomplete data. It is a fundamental step in data cleaning and is essential for maintaining data integrity. Imputing data allows you to preserve the overall structure of your dataset while making it suitable for analysis.

Python Code Example

Let's take a look at a simple Python example using the pandas library to perform data imputation. Suppose we have a dataset with missing values in a column named "Income." We'll impute these missing values with the mean income of the available data:

python

```
import pandas as pd

# Load your dataset
```

```
data = pd.read_csv('your_dataset.csv')

# Impute missing values in the 'Income' column with the mean
mean_income = data.mean()
data.fillna(mean_income, inplace=True)
```

This code reads a dataset, calculates the mean income, and fills missing values with this mean.

Data cleaning, with its focus on addressing missing data, outliers, and imputation, is a foundational skill in the journey of analyzing economic and financial data. It ensures that your results and models are reliable and trustworthy, setting the stage for more advanced econometric analysis in the chapters to come. Remember, the quality of your analysis often depends on the cleanliness of your data, and mastering data cleaning is a key step toward becoming a proficient data scientist and economist.

Data Transformation

Welcome to the heart of data preparation, where we venture into the realm of data transformation. In this section, we'll unravel the intricacies of shaping your data to make it more amenable for analysis and modeling, specifically focusing on normalization and feature engineering. These techniques are your tools for molding raw data into a refined masterpiece, ready for in-depth econometric exploration.

Normalization: Unveiling the Balance in Data

Normalization is the art of scaling your data, ensuring that it falls within a consistent range. This practice is pivotal, especially when dealing with features or variables that have differing scales or units. When variables are on significantly different scales, it can adversely affect the performance of certain machine learning algorithms. Normalization brings a sense of balance to the playing field, making it easier for your models to learn.

One of the most common normalization techniques is the Min-Max scaling, which scales data to a range of . Let's take a glance at how this technique can be implemented in Python:

python

```
from sklearn.preprocessing import MinMaxScaler

# Instantiate the scaler
scaler = MinMaxScaler()

# Fit and transform your data (assuming 'data' is a pandas DataFrame)
data_normalized = scaler.fit_transform(data)
```

Feature Engineering: Sculpting Your Data

Feature engineering is an artisanal process that involves creating new features or modifying existing ones to enhance the performance of your models. It's not just about working with data; it's about transforming it into a symphony of variables that can unveil valuable insights. Feature engineering can lead to more accurate predictions and better model interpretability.

Python Code Example - Feature Engineering

Suppose you have a dataset containing a date column, and you believe that the day of the week may influence your analysis. You can engineer a new feature by extracting the day of the week:

python

```
import pandas as pd

# Assuming you have a date column named 'Date'
data = data.dt.dayofweek
```

In this snippet, we've added a new feature, 'DayOfWeek,' that represents the day of the week. This feature could be valuable in econometric analysis, particularly when studying trends or cyclical patterns.

Feature engineering is a creative endeavor, where domain knowledge and intuition play a significant role. It's about uncovering hidden patterns and relationships within your data, often transforming it from a simple dataset into a valuable source of insights.

Crafting Data for Optimal Analysis

Data transformation is the art of preparing your dataset to meet the demands of rigorous analysis. Normalization ensures that your data is harmoniously scaled, while feature engineering enhances its expressive power. By using these techniques strategically, you can harness the true potential of your data, setting the stage for more advanced analysis in the chapters to come.

In the forthcoming chapters, we will delve into the fascinating world of econometric analysis, guided by your transformed data. From multiple linear regression to time series analysis, the tools we're building now will prove invaluable. So, sharpen your skills in data transformation, as they will be your most trusted allies on this econometric journey.

Data Visualization

In the intricate tapestry of data science and econometric analysis, there's a crucial thread that brings the patterns and insights to life - data visualization. In this chapter, we step into the fascinating realm of visual representation, where numbers transform into meaningful stories. We'll explore the power of Matplotlib and Seaborn, two Python libraries that serve as the artist's palette in this vivid canvas of data exploration.

Visualizing the Data Landscape

Why is data visualization so vital? Well, it's the bridge that connects raw data with human understanding. As an economist, you'll deal with vast datasets, complex relationships, and multifaceted trends. These are often challenging to decipher purely from numbers and statistics. This is where data visualization shines.

Matplotlib and Seaborn are your trusty companions on this journey. Matplotlib, a versatile plotting library, provides a vast toolkit for creating static, animated, or interactive visualizations. On the other hand, Seaborn, built on top of Matplotlib, specializes in creating aesthetically pleasing statistical graphics.

Python Code Example - Basic Plot

Let's start with a simple example using Matplotlib to create a line plot:

python

```
import matplotlib.pyplot as plt

# Sample data
x =
y =

# Create a line plot
plt.plot(x, y)

# Add labels
plt.xlabel('X-axis')
plt.ylabel('Y-axis')

# Display the plot
plt.show()
```

This basic example showcases how to create a line plot. You can customize it further by adding titles, legends, or changing the style to suit your preferences.

Beyond the Basics: Seaborn's Aesthetic Touch

While Matplotlib offers powerful flexibility, Seaborn adds an aesthetic layer to your visualizations. It's designed for creating statistically-informed, attractive plots with minimal coding effort.

Python Code Example - Seaborn's Distplot

Here's a simple example using Seaborn to create a histogram:

python

```
import seaborn as sns
import matplotlib.pyplot as plt

# Sample data
data =

# Create a histogram with Seaborn
sns.distplot(data, kde=False)

# Add labels
plt.xlabel('Values')
plt.ylabel('Frequency')
```

Display the plot

plt.show()

In this example, Seaborn's distplot makes it easy to create a histogram. You can also overlay a kernel density estimate (KDE) for a richer representation of the data distribution.

A Kaleidoscope of Possibilities

Your journey into data visualization doesn't stop here. Matplotlib and Seaborn offer a wide range of plot types, from scatter plots and bar charts to heatmaps and violin plots. The choice of visualization depends on your data and the story you want to tell.

These visualizations not only help you understand your data but also convey your findings to others. In the chapters ahead, you'll apply these visualization techniques to real-world datasets, illuminating complex economic phenomena and creating compelling narratives.

As an economist, the ability to visualize data is an essential skill. With Matplotlib and Seaborn as your companions, you have the tools to create engaging, informative, and insightful plots. In the next chapter, we'll put these skills to the test as we explore a real-world dataset, applying the principles of data preparation and visualization to unravel intriguing stories hidden within the numbers. So, gear up to translate data into visuals, for it's a language every economist must speak.

Real-world Data Case Study

Now that you've ventured through the intricacies of data preparation, it's time to put your newfound skills to the test. In this chapter, we'll delve into a real-world data case study, where the rubber meets the road. You'll apply the techniques you've learned and prepare a dataset, paving the way for deeper insights and meaningful analysis.

Data in the Wild

The world of economics thrives on real data—complex, messy, and diverse. To equip you with practical experience, we'll explore an actual dataset. This is where your knowledge of data types, cleaning, transformation, and visualization will shine. But first, let's set the stage for this case study.

Defining the Challenge

Imagine we're tasked with analyzing a dataset that contains retail sales data for a large chain of stores. Our goal is to understand sales trends, identify key factors influencing sales, and ultimately optimize performance. This is a typical econometric task where your Python skills will prove invaluable.

Python at the Helm

Before we dive into the dataset, we need to ensure our Python environment is ready. If you recall from Chapter 1.2b, you learned how to set up your Python environment. Now is the time to apply that knowledge. Install the necessary libraries, load your dataset into a Jupyter Notebook, and get ready to work your magic.

Python Code Example - Setting up the Environment

python

```python
# Import libraries
import pandas as pd
import matplotlib.pyplot as plt
import seaborn as sns

# Load the dataset
data = pd.read_csv('retail_sales_data.csv')

# Check the first few rows
data.head()
```

In this code, we use Pandas to read our dataset and Matplotlib along with Seaborn for visualization. By following the steps you've learned, you've established a strong foundation for working with real-world data.

Exploring the Data

Before any analysis, it's essential to understand your data. What columns are available? Are there any missing values? What's the distribution of key variables? Data exploration is your compass in this journey.

Python Code Example - Exploring the Data

python

```python
# Check data info
data.info()

# Check summary statistics
summary = data.describe()

# Visualize sales distribution
plt.figure(figsize=(10, 6))
sns.histplot(data, kde=True)
plt.title('Sales Distribution')
plt.show()
```

This code snippet provides an overview of your dataset, its structure, and basic statistics. Furthermore, it visualizes the distribution of sales, a crucial variable in our analysis.

Cleaning and Transformation

In Chapter 2.3b, you learned how to handle missing data, outliers, and perform data imputation. Now is the time to roll up your sleeves. Clean the data, ensuring it's ready for further analysis. This process might involve filling missing values, dealing with outliers, and feature engineering.

Python Code Example - Data Cleaning and Transformation

python

```python
# Handle missing values
data.fillna(0, inplace=True)
```

```
# Handle outliers
q1 = data.quantile(0.25)
q3 = data.quantile(0.75)
iqr = q3 - q1
lower_bound = q1 - 1.5 * iqr
upper_bound = q3 + 1.5 * iqr
data = data >= lower_bound) & (data <= upper_bound)

# Feature engineering
data = pd.to_datetime(data).dt.year
data = pd.to_datetime(data).dt.month

# Check the cleaned data
data.info()
```

This code showcases the data cleaning process. We fill missing values with zeros, address outliers, and introduce new features for analysis.

Visualizing Insights

In Chapter 2.5b, you learned the art of data visualization using Matplotlib and Seaborn. Now, apply these skills to gain insights from your dataset. Visualize the relationships between variables, trends over time, and any other patterns that might emerge.

Python Code Example - Visualizing Data Insights

python

```
# Visualize sales over time
plt.figure(figsize=(12, 6))
sns.lineplot(data=data, x='Year', y='Sales')
plt.title('Sales Trend Over Time')
plt.show()

# Visualize the relationship between sales and other variables
plt.figure(figsize=(12, 6))
sns.pairplot(data, vars=, kind='scatter')
plt.title('Relationships Between Sales, Advertising, and
Competitor Price')
plt.show()
```

These code snippets offer a glimpse of what's possible. You can visualize sales trends over time and explore relationships between sales, advertising, and competitor prices.

As you can see, a real-world data case study is a practical application of your Python skills. You've set up your environment, explored the data, cleaned and transformed it, and visualized key insights. This is the essence of econometric analysis.

The foundation you've laid in this chapter is pivotal. The next chapters will delve into more advanced econometric techniques and machine learning applications. You'll be well-prepared to tackle complex economic questions and extract valuable insights from data. The journey has just begun, and the possibilities are boundless.

Conclusion

In this chapter, you've taken your first steps into the world of real-world data analysis in econometrics. Armed with Python, you've set up your environment, explored a retail sales dataset, and harnessed data preparation techniques. This case study marked a pivotal moment in your journey.

You've learned how to clean and transform data, visualize insights, and set the stage for more advanced analysis. With each passing chapter, your proficiency in Python will grow, opening doors to deeper understanding and practical applications in the field of economics.

As we turn the page to the next chapter, you'll delve further into the intricacies of econometrics, exploring more advanced models, techniques, and real-world applications. It's a journey of discovery, and the next chapter holds the key to unlocking even greater insights. Get ready to embark on the next phase of your Python econometrics adventure.

CHAPTER 3: BASIC ECONOMETRIC ANALYSIS

Welcome to Chapter 3 of "Python in Econometrics: Bridging Data Science and Economic Analysis." In this chapter, we delve into the heart of econometrics, exploring the fundamental techniques that underpin economic analysis.

Econometric analysis is a powerful tool for economists, enabling us to model and interpret the relationships between variables and make informed predictions about economic phenomena. By combining Python's data manipulation capabilities with econometric principles, we equip ourselves with the tools needed to tackle real-world economic questions.

This chapter serves as a cornerstone for your econometric journey. We'll start by examining simple linear regression and multiple linear regression, fundamental concepts that form the foundation of modeling economic relationships. We'll explore how to diagnose and interpret these models, providing you with the ability to critically assess empirical economic data.

As we proceed, we'll transition from theory to practice. You'll apply these regression models to real-world datasets, bridging the gap between textbook knowledge and hands-on experience.

By the end of this chapter, you'll not only understand the principles of basic econometric analysis but also be able to utilize them effectively.

Our journey has already taken you through Python's setup, data preparation, and visualization. Now, you're poised to become a true econometrician, capable of analyzing economic phenomena with confidence. So, let's dive into the world of basic econometric analysis and discover how it empowers us to make sense of the economic forces that shape our world.

Simple Linear Regression: Unveiling The Foundation Of Econometrics

Simple linear regression, or SLR, lies at the heart of econometrics. It's the bedrock upon which more complex models are built, making it crucial for understanding economic relationships. In this section, we'll demystify the concept of SLR and guide you through its formulation and interpretation.

The Foundation of Simple Linear Regression

At its core, simple linear regression is a method that helps us understand how a dependent variable changes as a result of changes in a single independent variable. Imagine we want to explore the relationship between the price of a product and the quantity demanded. SLR provides us with the tools to analyze this connection.

The formula for SLR is elegant in its simplicity:

$$Y = \beta 0 + \beta 1 X + \varepsilon Y = \beta 0 + \beta 1 X + \varepsilon$$

Here's what each component represents:

Y is the dependent variable, which we want to predict or explain.

X is the independent variable, also known as the predictor.

β_0 is the intercept, representing the value of Y when X is zero.

β_1 is the slope, indicating how Y changes with a one-unit change in X.

ε is the error term, accounting for the random variability we can't explain with the model.

This formula allows us to create a line that best fits the data points, making it a valuable tool for understanding relationships between variables.

Interpreting the Model

Once we've established the model, interpreting it becomes the next step. This interpretation often revolves around understanding the values of β_0 and β_1.

β_0 represents the point where the regression line crosses the Y-axis. In our product price example, this could be the expected quantity demanded when the price is zero. But keep in mind that this interpretation might not always make sense in real-world scenarios.

β_1 holds the key to the slope of the line. It tells us how the quantity demanded changes for each one-unit increase in price. A positive β_1 indicates that an increase in price leads to a decrease in quantity demanded, while a negative β_1 suggests the opposite.

The sign and magnitude of β_1 provide critical insights into the direction and strength of the relationship between variables. A larger magnitude of $\beta_1\beta_1$ suggests a more substantial impact of XX on YY.

Python Implementation

Let's put theory into practice. We can employ Python to perform SLR effortlessly. We'll use libraries like NumPy and SciPy to conduct the regression analysis and Matplotlib for visualization. Here's a simplified example:

python

```
import numpy as np
from scipy import stats
import matplotlib.pyplot as plt

# Sample data
X = np.array()
Y = np.array()

# Perform linear regression
slope, intercept, r_value, p_value, std_err = stats.linregress(X, Y)

# Create a regression line
regression_line = slope * X + intercept

# Visualize the data and regression line
plt.scatter(X, Y, label="Data Points")
plt.plot(X, regression_line, label="Regression Line", color='red')
plt.xlabel("X")
```

```
plt.ylabel("Y")
plt.legend()
plt.show()

# Interpret the results
print(f"Slope (β₁): {slope}")
print(f"Intercept (β₀): {intercept}")
print(f"R-squared value: {r_value ** 2}")
```

The Python example above calculates the regression line, plots it along with the data points, and interprets the results.

The Power of Simple Linear Regression

As we wrap up our discussion on simple linear regression, remember that it forms the cornerstone of econometrics. Its power lies in its ability to provide insights into the relationship between two variables, paving the way for more complex models. Whether you're exploring the impact of price on demand or any other economic phenomenon, SLR equips you with the foundational knowledge you need.

Multiple Linear Regression

In our journey through the realm of Python in econometrics, we now find ourselves delving into the intricacies of multiple linear regression. If you recall, in the previous section, we discussed simple linear regression and gained insight into the foundation of regression analysis. Now, it's time to broaden our horizons and explore how we can model more complex relationships between variables.

The Beauty of Multiple Linear Regression

Multiple linear regression is a powerful extension of simple linear regression. While simple linear regression helps us understand the linear relationship between two variables, multiple linear regression steps up the game by accommodating multiple predictor variables. This is incredibly useful when dealing with real-world scenarios where various factors can influence an outcome.

Let's dive deeper into the core components:

Model Building: At the heart of multiple linear regression is the construction of a mathematical model. This model is a representation of the relationship between a dependent variable (the one you want to predict) and multiple independent variables (the factors that might influence the dependent variable). In this section, we'll guide you through the art of model building, explaining how to choose the right independent variables and how to set up the equation.

Assumptions: Like any statistical method, multiple linear regression comes with its own set of assumptions. These assumptions are the backbone of the technique, and understanding them is crucial for meaningful analysis. We'll walk you through these assumptions, which include linearity, independence, normality, and homoscedasticity. You'll learn how to assess whether your data meets these assumptions and what to do if they aren't satisfied.

Multicollinearity: It's not uncommon for independent variables to be correlated with one another, and this can create complications in multiple linear regression. Multicollinearity refers to high correlations among independent variables. We'll explore why multicollinearity is a problem and how you can detect and mitigate it.

Interpreting the Coefficients: The coefficients in a multiple linear regression model hold valuable information. They represent the strength and direction of the relationships between the independent variables and the dependent variable. Understanding how to interpret these coefficients is essential to gain insights from your model.

Modeling Techniques: We'll also introduce you to various modeling techniques and strategies. This includes methods to identify and remove irrelevant independent variables, model selection processes, and strategies for dealing with categorical predictors.

Applications: As with every section of this book, we'll provide you with real-world applications. These examples will showcase the practical use of multiple linear regression in economic analysis, from predicting housing prices to evaluating the impact of advertising campaigns.

Now, let's shed some light on the intricacies of each of these components.

Model Building:

Building a multiple linear regression model requires careful consideration of which variables to include. The process involves selecting independent variables based on your understanding of the subject matter and the goals of your analysis. You'll learn how to specify your model, define your dependent variable, and determine the right predictors.

Assumptions:

Understanding and validating the assumptions of multiple linear regression are essential for confident analysis. These assumptions include:

Linearity: The relationships between the independent variables and the dependent variable are linear.

Independence: Observations are independent of each other. The value of the dependent variable for one observation should not depend on the values of the independent variables for other observations.

Normality: The residuals (the differences between the observed and predicted values) are normally distributed.

Homoscedasticity: The variance of the residuals should be constant across all values of the independent variables.

We'll show you how to test these assumptions and what to do if they are violated.

Multicollinearity:

Multicollinearity arises when independent variables are highly correlated, which can lead to unstable coefficient estimates. We'll delve into techniques for detecting multicollinearity and how to address it by selecting the right set of predictors.

Interpreting the Coefficients:

Interpreting coefficients is where the real magic happens. We'll guide you through the process of understanding what each coefficient means and how to interpret their values.

Modeling Techniques:

As you explore the world of multiple linear regression, you'll encounter various modeling techniques. We'll provide you with a toolbox of methods to choose the best set of predictors, handle categorical variables, and decide on the model's complexity.

Applications:

Finally, as we've done throughout this book, we'll tie everything together with practical applications. You'll see how multiple linear regression is used in real-world economic analysis, making it clear how the theory translates into actionable insights.

By the end of this section, you'll be well-equipped to tackle complex economic problems, model intricate relationships between variables, and make informed decisions using Python and econometrics. Stay tuned for more, as our journey through this data-driven adventure continues.

3.3b Regression Diagnostics (1,100 words): Explain diagnostic tests such as residuals analysis and influential points.

Welcome to the fascinating world of regression diagnostics.

In this section, we will delve into the crucial aspects of understanding the health of your multiple linear regression model. Just like a physician diagnoses a patient's ailment, you, as an aspiring data scientist or economist, will diagnose the health of your regression model to ensure its reliability and accuracy.

Residuals Analysis: Peering into the Soul of Your Model

Imagine the predictions made by your regression model as a path, and the actual data points as the terrain. Your goal is to ensure that your model's path aligns with the terrain as closely as possible. Residuals analysis provides you with the tools to achieve this alignment.

What Are Residuals?

In the context of regression analysis, residuals are the differences between the actual observed values and the values predicted by the model. These residuals contain valuable information about the model's performance. Positive residuals indicate that your model underpredicts the actual values, while negative residuals mean overprediction.

Why Residuals Matter

Residuals are like the breadcrumbs left behind by your model on its journey through data. Analyzing these breadcrumbs allows you to assess the model's assumptions and detect any patterns or anomalies that may have been missed.

Understanding Residual Plots

Residual plots are a powerful tool for visualizing the

relationship between independent variables and the residuals. In a well-behaved model, these plots should exhibit randomness. However, patterns or trends in the residuals can signal issues with the model. We will discuss various types of residual plots, such as:

Residuals vs. Fitted Values: This plot helps you examine whether the residuals have a consistent spread across the range of predicted values. It's also a tool for identifying outliers and influential points.

Normal Q-Q Plot: This plot assesses whether the residuals follow a normal distribution. Deviations from a straight line can indicate non-normality.

Scale-Location Plot: This plot helps you check whether the spread of residuals remains constant as the predicted values change. A non-constant spread suggests heteroscedasticity, which violates one of the regression assumptions.

Residuals vs. Leverage: Leverage points are observations that have the potential to significantly impact the regression coefficients. This plot identifies those points and helps you evaluate their influence.

Dealing with Influential Points

Influential points are observations that can significantly affect the regression results. These points can distort the regression equation, coefficients, and predictions. In this section, we will explore techniques to identify and manage influential points. Methods like Cook's distance and DFFITS can help you flag potential troublemakers.

Leaving No Stone Unturned

A skilled data scientist or economist leaves no stone unturned when assessing the reliability of a regression model. Beyond residual analysis and influential points, there are other crucial diagnostics to explore, such as:

Variance Inflation Factor (VIF): VIF quantifies how much the variance of the estimated regression coefficients is increased due to multicollinearity. High VIF values indicate problematic multicollinearity.

Heteroscedasticity Tests: These tests determine whether the variance of the residuals is consistent across different levels of the independent variables. We'll delve into techniques like the Breusch-Pagan test or the White test to diagnose and remedy heteroscedasticity.

Autocorrelation: For time series data, autocorrelation diagnostics help identify dependencies between observations at different time points.

Unraveling the Threads of Model Interpretation

In the intricate tapestry of econometrics and data science, the "Model Interpretation" phase is akin to deciphering the intricate patterns within. This section is your guide to the art and science of understanding what your regression model is trying to convey.

The Key to Unlocking Knowledge

As you venture further into the realm of multiple linear regression, you'll find yourself swimming in a sea of coefficients, p-values, and statistical significance. These numbers are not mere abstractions but are your tools for extracting valuable insights from your data.

Deciphering the Coefficients

The coefficients in a multiple linear regression model play a pivotal role in defining the relationships between your independent variables and the target variable. Each coefficient corresponds to a specific independent variable, and it quantifies the change in the target variable for a one-unit change in the respective independent variable, keeping all other variables constant.

For instance, if you're examining the factors influencing housing prices, a coefficient for the number of bedrooms might indicate how much the price changes for each additional bedroom.

Assessing the Significance

Not all coefficients are created equal. Some may have a profound impact on the target variable, while others are mere whispers in the equation. Here's where p-values step in. P-values tell you whether the observed relationship between an independent variable and the target variable is statistically significant. In essence, they help you distinguish between noise and real signals.

Typically, a lower p-value (usually below 0.05) suggests that the variable is statistically significant and contributes meaningfully to the model. A higher p-value indicates that the variable may not be necessary for explaining the variance in the target variable.

Beware of Multicollinearity

In your journey, you may encounter multicollinearity, a phenomenon where independent variables in your model are highly correlated. This can muddy the waters of interpretation. Imagine trying to pinpoint which of your two compasses is pointing north when they consistently give the same reading.

Multicollinearity can make it challenging to isolate the individual effects of correlated variables. When dealing with multicollinearity, your interpretation must tread carefully and consider the broader context of the model.

Validation and Real-world Application

Interpretation isn't a solitary endeavor. It should work in harmony with validation and application. This trifecta ensures the robustness of your model and its practical utility.

Validation techniques, such as cross-validation and goodness-of-fit tests, help assess the model's predictive power and generalizability. They offer a reality check, showing how well your model fares when facing new data.

But the true test of your model's prowess lies in its real-world applications. The value of your interpretation becomes evident when you employ your model in concrete scenarios. Whether it's predicting stock prices, estimating the impact of policy changes, or understanding customer behavior, the real-world applications provide a litmus test for your model's insights.

The Crucial Need for Validation

Your journey began with an exploration of simple and multiple linear regressions, learning about the fundamental theories, assumptions, and math behind the models. Now, it's time to make sure these models aren't just abstract constructs but practical tools for making informed decisions.

Model validation is the litmus test. It's the process of scrutinizing your models to ensure they're not merely overfitting your training data but can also generalize to new, unseen data. You see, models have a knack for capturing every nuance in the data they're trained on, but our goal is to make them general enough to make accurate predictions in various situations.

To perform model validation, techniques like cross-validation come into play. Cross-validation is like a series of rehearsals before the grand performance. It helps you evaluate your model's performance on different subsets of your data, ensuring that it's not overly dependent on one specific set.

The Real-world Application - Bridging Theory and Practice

The real-world dataset you'll explore serves as the bridge between theoretical concepts and tangible results. It's one thing to understand the intricacies of regression models on paper, but it's quite another to put that knowledge to practical use.

Imagine being tasked with forecasting stock prices, estimating the impact of policy changes, or understanding consumer behavior. These are the real-world conundrums that econometricians tackle, and in this chapter, you get a taste of what it's like to be in their shoes.

Python in Action - Example and Application

Let's bring Python to life with a practical example. Consider a scenario where you're working with a dataset of historical stock prices. You've built a multiple linear regression model that aims to predict future stock prices based on various factors like historical performance, trading volume, and macroeconomic indicators.

To validate this model, you employ a technique known as k-fold cross-validation. It involves splitting your dataset into 'k' subsets, training the model on 'k-1' subsets, and testing it on the remaining one. You repeat this process 'k' times, each time using a different subset as the test set. This way, you ensure that your model's performance is consistent across different portions of the data.

Your model might perform exceptionally well on your training data, but cross-validation will reveal its true mettle when confronted with previously unseen data. Only then can you be confident in its ability to make accurate predictions in the real world.

Python Programming Example

Step 1: Importing Libraries

We begin by importing the necessary libraries. Scikit-learn provides excellent tools for model validation and cross-validation.

python

```
import numpy as np
import pandas as pd
from sklearn.model_selection import cross_val_score, train_test_split
from sklearn.linear_model import LinearRegression
```

Step 2: Creating Sample Data

Let's create some sample data. For this example, we'll generate synthetic data for simplicity. In practice, you would use your real-world dataset.

python

```
# Generate synthetic data
np.random.seed(42)
X = np.random.rand(100, 1) # Independent variable
y = 2 * X + 1 + 0.1 * np.random.randn(100) # Dependent variable
with some noise
```

Step 3: Splitting Data

We split the data into training and testing sets. In practice, this step is crucial to validate the model's performance.

python

```
# Split the data into training and testing sets
```

```python
X_train, X_test, y_train, y_test = train_test_split(X, y,
test_size=0.2, random_state=42)
```

Step 4: Model Training

Now, let's train a simple linear regression model on the training data.

python

```python
# Create a linear regression model
model = LinearRegression()

# Train the model
model.fit(X_train, y_train)
```

Step 5: Model Validation Using Cross-Validation

Here's where we perform model validation using cross-validation. We'll use the cross_val_score function to evaluate the model's performance.

python

```python
# Perform cross-validation (let's say k=5 for 5-fold cross-validation)
scores = cross_val_score(model, X, y, cv=5, scoring='r2')

# Display the cross-validation scores
print("Cross-validation scores:", scores)
print("Mean R-squared:", scores.mean())
```

In this example, we use R-squared (coefficient of determination) as the scoring metric, which measures the goodness of fit of the model. The cross_val_score function splits the data into 'k' subsets, trains and tests the model on each subset, and returns the R-squared scores for each fold. We then calculate the mean R-squared value as a measure of the model's overall performance.

This Python example demonstrates the essential steps in model validation, and you can adapt it to your own datasets and regression models. Remember that in practice, you'd replace the synthetic data with your real-world data for meaningful validation.

Conclusion

In this chapter, we delved into the critical phase of model validation, a cornerstone of any sound econometric analysis. Validating our regression models is akin to ensuring the tools in a skilled craftsman's toolbox are sharpened and ready for use. It's a process that assures us our models are capable of making reliable predictions.

We began by introducing the concept of cross-validation, a technique that assesses a model's performance across different subsets of data, thereby reducing the risk of overfitting. Through cross-validation, we gauged the robustness of our regression models, and in doing so, gained insights into their predictive capabilities.

The R-squared scores provided us with a quantitative measure of the goodness of fit, helping us understand how well our models explain the variability in the data. This evaluation equips us to discern whether our models are merely overfitting the training data or if they generalize well to new, unseen data.

CHAPTER 4: TIME SERIES ANALYSIS

Welcome to Chapter 4 of our journey through Python in Econometrics. As we venture further into the realm of data science and economic analysis, we arrive at a fascinating crossroads where the dimension of time takes center stage. Time series data, a cornerstone of economic analysis, exhibits intricate patterns and dynamics that have a profound impact on decision-making in various fields.

In this chapter, we embark on a comprehensive exploration of Time Series Analysis. The ability to understand and harness the insights hidden within time-dependent data is a prized skill for economists, financial analysts, and data scientists alike. We will unravel the intricacies of time series data, delve into the concepts of stationarity and autocorrelation, and equip you with the tools to make informed predictions and forecasts.

Our journey begins with an "Introduction to Time Series Data," where we will lay the foundation by defining and understanding the unique characteristics of time series data. We will explore the nature of temporal patterns and how they influence economic phenomena, from stock market trends to macroeconomic indicators.

Moving forward, we will introduce "Time Series

Decomposition," a technique that allows us to break down complex time series data into its constituent components, such as trend, seasonality, and noise. This deconstruction empowers us to understand the underlying drivers of a time series, thereby enhancing our forecasting capabilities.

In "Moving Averages," we explore how to smoothen time series data to uncover underlying trends and patterns. We will delve into various moving average techniques that are invaluable for identifying turning points and making predictions based on historical data.

A significant highlight of this chapter is the introduction of ARIMA (AutoRegressive Integrated Moving Average) Models in "ARIMA Models." This powerful framework for time series analysis provides us with the tools to model, estimate, and forecast time series data accurately. We will cover the model identification process, parameter estimation, and delve into forecasting using ARIMA models.

And finally, in a real-world context, we'll apply our newly acquired time series analysis skills to a "Real-world Forecasting Case Study." Here, we'll predict stock prices, showcasing how this knowledge can be practically applied in domains where accurate predictions are of paramount importance.

This chapter is your gateway to unlocking the secrets of temporal data and harnessing its predictive potential. As we navigate through time series analysis, you'll gain a profound understanding of economic dynamics, enabling you to make more informed decisions, whether in finance, policy, or business. So, let's embark on this exciting journey through time and discover the patterns that shape our world.

Introduction to Time Series Data

Let's start by understanding the core concepts of time series data. Time series data is a sequence of observations taken at equally spaced intervals over time. This data type captures the evolution of a variable or phenomenon as it unfolds chronologically. Imagine stock prices over weeks, monthly unemployment rates, or yearly GDP growth. These are all examples of time series data, and Python equips us to dissect and extract valuable insights from them.

One of the fundamental properties we encounter in time series data is stationarity. Stationarity implies that statistical properties, such as the mean and variance, remain constant over time. In simpler terms, it's as if the data dances around a fixed point without any consistent trend. Why does this matter? Stationarity simplifies the analysis, making it easier to model and predict future values. Python libraries like NumPy and pandas are your trusty companions in checking and achieving stationarity by employing techniques such as differencing and transforming data.

Decompose time series data into trend, seasonality, and noise components

Imagine you're observing the daily stock prices of a prominent tech company. The graph appears erratic, with prices rising and falling. But how do you make sense of this seemingly chaotic data? The answer lies in time series decomposition, a technique that helps us break down the data into its fundamental components. In this section, we'll delve into the fascinating world of decomposing time series data using Python, unlocking valuable insights for forecasting and analysis.

At the heart of time series decomposition are three key components: trend, seasonality, and noise. Think of them as the essential building blocks of your time series data.

Firstly, we have the trend component. The trend represents the underlying pattern or long-term direction in the data. It helps us discern whether the stock prices are generally increasing, decreasing, or remaining stable over time. Python's libraries like NumPy and pandas provide tools for trend analysis, allowing you to extract this valuable information.

For instance, if you notice that stock prices have been consistently rising over several years, this indicates an upward trend. Conversely, if there's a consistent decline, it signals a downward trend. Accurate identification of the trend component is vital in making informed investment decisions or predicting future economic indicators.

Next, we encounter seasonality. Seasonality captures regular, recurring patterns within the data, often associated with specific time periods. An example could be the surge in retail sales during the holiday season or the monthly fluctuations in heating oil consumption during winter. Python's libraries like statsmodels and seasonal decomposition of time series (STL) can help us tease apart these cyclical patterns.

By identifying seasonality in your data, you gain a more profound understanding of the factors influencing your time series. For instance, recognizing that a product's sales peak every year in the summer months can be invaluable for inventory management or marketing strategies.

The third component is noise, often referred to as "error" or "residual." Noise represents the irregular and seemingly random fluctuations within the data. It's the part of the time series that's not attributed to trend or seasonality. In essence, it's the unpredictable aspect of your data. Python's statistical libraries, like SciPy, come in handy for isolating and quantifying this noise.

Understanding noise allows you to assess the level of unpredictability in your data. In financial modeling, for instance, this knowledge can be vital for risk assessment. Recognizing when your stock price data is predominantly driven by noise rather than an actual trend or seasonality pattern can prevent investment decisions based on misleading signals.

Now, let's put theory into practice with a simple Python example. Consider a dataset representing monthly sales of ice cream over several years. Using Python's libraries, you can decompose this time series into its trend, seasonality, and noise components. Once you've extracted these components, you'll gain deeper insights into how the business is performing.

python

```python
import pandas as pd
import statsmodels.api as sm
import matplotlib.pyplot as plt

# Load your time series data (replace 'data.csv' with your dataset)
data = pd.read_csv('data.csv')
data = pd.to_datetime(data)
data.set_index('Month', inplace=True)
```

```
# Decompose the time series
result = sm.tsa.seasonal_decompose(data, model='additive')

# Plot the components
fig, (ax1, ax2, ax3, ax4) = plt.subplots(4, 1, figsize=(10, 8))
ax1.set_title('Observed')
ax1.plot(data)
ax2.set_title('Trend')
ax2.plot(result.trend)
ax3.set_title('Seasonal')
ax3.plot(result.seasonal)
ax4.set_title('Residual')
ax4.plot(result.resid)

plt.tight_layout()
plt.show()
```

This Python code snippet uses the statsmodels library to perform seasonal decomposition on your time series data, providing a visual representation of the trend, seasonality, and noise components. By examining these components, you can make more informed decisions, whether it's about adjusting your production schedule for ice cream or fine-tuning your investment strategy.

Moving Averages

Welcome to the enthralling world of moving averages, a powerful tool in the arsenal of an econometrician. While the concept of an average might seem elementary, moving averages offer a nuanced approach to understanding and forecasting time series data. In this section, we will dive deep into moving averages, how they work, and why they are an indispensable component of time series analysis.

Moving averages, in essence, are the cornerstone of smoothing techniques. They help us extract underlying trends from noisy time series data, making it easier to discern patterns, fluctuations, and important turning points.

But what exactly is a moving average? In simple terms, it's a calculated average of a series of data points, shifting through time. Each moving average value represents a set of data points within a given window. These averages "move" through the data, providing a smoothed representation of the underlying trends.

Now, let's break down the two primary types of moving averages you'll encounter: Simple Moving Averages (SMA) and Exponential Moving Averages (EMA).

Simple Moving Averages (SMA): This is the more straightforward of the two. SMAs assign equal weight to each data point within the moving average window. To calculate an SMA, you add up the values within the window and divide by the number of data points. This method ensures that every point within the window contributes equally to the average.

Consider a 10-day SMA applied to daily stock prices. On each day, it considers the past 10 days of prices, sums them up, and divides by 10 to get the moving average for that day. It creates a smoothed curve that filters out day-to-day noise, making it easier to identify trends.

Exponential Moving Averages (EMA): EMAs, on the other hand,

assign more weight to recent data points. This means that the EMA is more responsive to recent changes, making it an excellent choice for those interested in quickly spotting emerging trends. The EMA calculation involves more complex mathematical formulas, but Python's libraries like pandas make it easy to compute.

Moving averages are invaluable for detecting trends, seasonal patterns, and irregular movements within your data. They are particularly useful when you want to reduce noise in a dataset, which can obscure real trends.

Here's an example to illustrate the power of moving averages. Imagine you're analyzing monthly sales data for a retail store. You observe that the sales data has high variability, making it challenging to identify long-term trends. Applying a simple moving average over a 12-month window, you'll begin to see a much smoother curve, highlighting the general direction of sales. It helps you determine whether sales are rising, falling, or remaining relatively stable.

Now, let's shift our focus to the practical side of moving averages. Python, with its data manipulation and visualization libraries, provides a seamless platform for implementing moving averages. Here's a simple code snippet to calculate and visualize a 30-day SMA for a hypothetical stock price dataset:

```python
import pandas as pd
import matplotlib.pyplot as plt

# Load your time series data (replace 'data.csv' with your dataset)
```

```python
data = pd.read_csv('data.csv')
data = pd.to_datetime(data)
data.set_index('Date', inplace=True)

# Calculate the 30-day Simple Moving Average
sma_30 = data.rolling(window=30).mean()

# Plot the original data and the moving average
plt.figure(figsize=(12, 6))
plt.plot(data.index, data, label='Original Data', color='blue')
plt.plot(data.index, sma_30, label='30-day SMA', color='red')
plt.xlabel('Date')
plt.ylabel('Price')
plt.legend()
plt.title('Stock Price and 30-day SMA')
plt.show()
```

In this example, you load your stock price data, calculate the 30-day SMA, and plot both the original data and the moving average. This visual representation offers a clear perspective on how moving averages can help you understand the underlying trend.

Moving averages are just one piece of the puzzle in the realm of time series analysis. In the upcoming sections of this book, we'll explore more advanced techniques, such as ARIMA models, which leverage moving averages as part of their forecasting process. So, stay with us as we continue our journey through the world of Python in econometrics.

ARIMA Models

In the ever-changing landscape of econometrics, one tool has stood the test of time, consistently proving its worth in the realm of time series analysis: ARIMA. The acronym, ARIMA, stands for AutoRegressive Integrated Moving Average, which might sound intimidating at first, but by the end of this section, you'll find yourself well-acquainted with its power and potential.

Understanding the ARIMA Model

The ARIMA model is like a Swiss Army knife for time series data. It's incredibly versatile, capable of capturing various patterns, whether they exhibit trends, seasonality, or complex dependencies. But what does each part of the acronym represent?

AutoRegressive (AR): This component models the relationship between the current data point and its past values. In essence, it accounts for the idea that future values are influenced by previous values. An AR term identifies how many past values are involved in predicting the future.

Integrated (I): This part deals with the differencing of the time series data. It's a critical step to make the data stationary, as ARIMA works best with stationary data. Stationary data simplifies the task of modeling as it ensures that statistical properties like mean, variance, and autocorrelation remain constant over time.

Moving Average (MA): MA, in ARIMA, refers to the dependency between a data point and a linear combination of past white noise error terms. It helps account for the sudden, unpredictable shocks in data.

Key Steps in ARIMA Modeling

Now, let's delve into the practical aspect of implementing ARIMA modeling. You'll often find yourself performing the following key steps:

1. Model Identification: The first step involves identifying the orders of the ARIMA model, namely p, d, and q.

p (AR order): The number of lag observations included in the model.

d (Integrated order): The number of times differencing is needed to make the data stationary.

q (MA order): The size of the moving average window.

Identifying these parameters is both an art and a science. Python's statsmodels library provides you with tools to estimate these values based on the Autocorrelation Function (ACF) and Partial Autocorrelation Function (PACF) plots.

2. Estimation: With the model orders determined, you can proceed to estimate the model. This step involves fitting the ARIMA model to your time series data. Python provides

robust libraries for this, making the estimation process straightforward.

3. Forecasting: Once you've successfully estimated the ARIMA model, you can use it to make future predictions. This is where ARIMA shines, as it provides you with a framework to forecast data points based on the model's understanding of the data's past behavior.

Python Code Example:

Let's walk through a simple Python code example to estimate and forecast a hypothetical time series dataset using ARIMA. We'll assume you've already imported the required libraries and loaded your data.

python

```
from statsmodels.tsa.arima_model import ARIMA

# Identify the orders p, d, and q
p = 1  # Example value
d = 1  # Example value
q = 1  # Example value

# Create and fit the ARIMA model
model = ARIMA(data, order=(p, d, q))
model_fit = model.fit()

# Make a one-step forecast
forecast = model_fit.forecast(steps=1)
```

```
# Print the forecasted value
print("Forecasted Value:", forecast)
```

This code is a simplified example. In practice, you would explore your data, create ACF and PACF plots, and iterate on different orders to fine-tune your model.

The ARIMA Advantage

ARIMA modeling has been a cornerstone of time series analysis for decades because of its flexibility and adaptability. It allows you to work with diverse types of time series data and provides a structured methodology for model identification, estimation, and forecasting.

But remember, ARIMA is just one part of the time series analysis toolkit. As you progress through this book, you'll encounter more advanced techniques and real-world case studies that leverage ARIMA models as part of a broader strategy to gain insights into economic and financial data.

Now that you've had your first introduction to ARIMA modeling, you're well-equipped to continue your journey through the world of Python in econometrics. The forecasted future awaits, full of economic insights and data-driven decision-making.

Real-world Forecasting Case Study (1,000 words): Apply ARIMA modeling to a real-world case for stock price forecasting.

Welcome to the real-world application of ARIMA modeling in econometrics. We've covered the foundations, delving into time series data, decomposition, moving averages, and the intricacies of ARIMA modeling. Now, let's put this knowledge to the test with a practical example – forecasting stock prices.

Stock price forecasting is an essential task in finance and investment. Accurate predictions can potentially translate into better investment decisions, higher returns, and a competitive edge in the market. Here, we'll walk through a case study that demonstrates how Python, combined with ARIMA, can be a powerful tool for such predictions.

Setting the Stage: Selecting a Stock

To start our forecasting journey, we need historical stock price data. For this case study, we'll choose a well-known company – let's say, Apple Inc. (AAPL). Historical stock price data for AAPL can be obtained from various financial data providers or through Python libraries such as yfinance.

Collecting Data:

Before we dive into ARIMA, we'll need historical data to work with. Python makes this process straightforward. Here's how you can collect historical AAPL stock price data:

python

```
import yfinance as yf

# Define the stock symbol (AAPL for Apple Inc.)
symbol = "AAPL"

# Define the start and end dates for data collection
```

```
start_date = "2010-01-01"
end_date = "2021-12-31"

# Fetch historical data
stock_data    =    yf.download(symbol,    start=start_date,
end=end_date)
```

In this code, we use the yfinance library to download historical data for AAPL from January 1, 2010, to December 31, 2021.

Exploring the Data:

Once you have the data, it's crucial to perform an initial exploration. This includes visualizing the historical stock prices, understanding trends, and identifying potential outliers.

python

```
import matplotlib.pyplot as plt

# Plotting historical stock prices
plt.figure(figsize=(12, 6))
plt.plot(stock_data, label='AAPL Closing Price', color='blue')
plt.title('AAPL Historical Stock Prices')
plt.xlabel('Date')
plt.ylabel('Price')
plt.legend()
plt.show()
```

This code snippet uses matplotlib to create a line plot of the closing prices. Visualizing the data helps you grasp the stock's past behavior and provides valuable insights for forecasting.

Applying ARIMA:

With the data in hand, it's time to apply ARIMA for stock price forecasting. First, you'll need to determine the ARIMA orders (p, d, q) based on the characteristics of your data. This often involves analyzing the autocorrelation and partial autocorrelation plots.

Once you've identified the orders, you can proceed with fitting the ARIMA model and generating forecasts:

python

```
from statsmodels.tsa.arima_model import ARIMA

# Example ARIMA orders (p, d, q)
p, d, q = 1, 1, 1

# Create and fit the ARIMA model
model = ARIMA(stock_data, order=(p, d, q))
model_fit = model.fit(disp=0)

# Make one-year-ahead forecasts
forecast_steps = 252  # Assuming 252 trading days in a year
forecast,          stderr,          conf_int          =
model_fit.forecast(steps=forecast_steps)
```

In this code, we've chosen an arbitrary order for illustration. In practice, you'd refine this by analyzing your specific data. The code also forecasts one year ahead (252 trading days).

Evaluating the Forecasts:

Once you've made forecasts, it's crucial to evaluate their accuracy. You can use metrics like Mean Absolute Error (MAE), Mean Squared Error (MSE), and Root Mean Squared Error (RMSE) to assess the model's performance.

python

```
from sklearn.metrics import mean_absolute_error, mean_squared_error
import numpy as np

# True stock prices for the one-year-ahead period
true_prices = stock_data

# Calculate MAE and RMSE
mae = mean_absolute_error(true_prices, forecast)
mse = mean_squared_error(true_prices, forecast)
rmse = np.sqrt(mse)
```

Visualizing the Results:

To provide a clear understanding of the model's performance, you can visualize the actual stock prices and the predicted values.

python

```
plt.figure(figsize=(12, 6))
plt.plot(true_prices, label='True Prices', color='blue')
plt.plot(forecast, label='Forecasted Prices', color='red')
plt.title('AAPL Stock Price Forecast')
plt.xlabel('Trading Days')
plt.ylabel('Price')
plt.legend()
plt.show()
```

Stock price forecasting is just one application of ARIMA modeling in the realm of econometrics. By following the steps outlined in this case study, you can apply ARIMA to various financial time series data, gaining insights that may aid your investment decisions.

Remember, successful forecasting goes beyond just one-time predictions. Continuous monitoring, model refinement, and staying informed about financial market trends are essential for building an effective investment strategy. Python and econometrics offer a powerful combination for this purpose, and by mastering these tools, you can make data-driven decisions in the dynamic world of finance.

Conclusion:

In this chapter, we embarked on a journey into the world of time series analysis and ARIMA modeling in the context of econometrics. We started with the foundational concepts, exploring time series data, decomposition, moving averages, and ARIMA models.

Our real-world forecasting case study demonstrated how Python, coupled with ARIMA, can be a powerful tool for predicting stock prices. We collected historical data, delved into ARIMA modeling, made one-year-ahead forecasts, and evaluated the model's performance.

This case study is but one example of the extensive applications of ARIMA modeling in econometrics. It showcases the potential of harnessing Python and econometric techniques for making data-driven financial decisions.

As we venture into the next chapter, we'll transition from time series analysis to panel data analysis, exploring the unique dynamics of panel datasets and the econometric methods employed to derive insights from them. With the foundation laid in this chapter, you're well-equipped to embrace the challenges and opportunities of panel data analysis. So, let's delve into this fascinating domain in Chapter 5, where we'll unlock the power of panel data for comprehensive economic analysis.

CHAPTER 5: PANEL DATA ANALYSIS

Greetings to Chapter 5 in "Python in Econometrics: Bridging Data Science and Economic Analysis." Within this chapter, we embark on a journey into the world of panel data analysis, a crucial discipline in the realm of econometrics. Here, we explore the complexities of panel datasets and the robust econometric techniques employed to uncover valuable insights from them.

Panel data, also known as longitudinal or cross-sectional time series data, offers a unique perspective that combines the strengths of both time series and cross-sectional data. It enables us to analyze the behavior of entities (individuals, firms, countries, etc.) over time while considering the variability across entities. This dual dimensionality opens doors to an array of research questions, from examining individual-level variations to exploring general trends over time.

The versatility of panel data makes it a preferred choice in many empirical studies, particularly in economics and social sciences. Researchers use it to explore the impact of policies, analyze economic trends, and gain a deeper understanding of the dynamics of various phenomena. By utilizing panel data, we can uncover patterns and relationships that might remain hidden when using other data structures.

In this chapter, we will equip you with the tools and knowledge needed to work with panel data effectively. We begin by unraveling the fundamentals, defining what panel data is and how it differs from other data types. You will gain an understanding of the structure, advantages, and potential challenges associated with panel datasets.

As we progress, we will explore different models commonly used in panel data analysis. Fixed effects models, random effects models, and dynamic panel data models will be in the spotlight, each with its unique applications and estimation methods. We will delve into endogeneity issues and the techniques available to test and address these concerns.

The chapter culminates with an empirical research case study, where we will apply panel data analysis to real-world data. This practical exercise will not only reinforce your understanding but also demonstrate the power of panel data in informing important decisions and policies.

Whether you're a budding economist or a seasoned data scientist, this chapter will provide you with valuable insights and skills to navigate the world of panel data analysis. Let's begin this journey into the realm of rich, multi-dimensional data that has the potential to uncover hidden truths and contribute to informed decision-making.

Understanding Panel Data

In our journey through the world of Python in econometrics, we now stand at the gateway of panel data analysis, a domain that holds immense potential for illuminating economic phenomena. To embark on this chapter successfully, we must first understand the very foundation upon which it rests—panel data itself.

At its core, panel data, sometimes referred to as longitudinal or cross-sectional time series data, is a unique and powerful data structure that combines elements of both time series and cross-sectional data. It adds a temporal dimension to our analysis by collecting observations across different entities (which can be individuals, firms, countries, or any other relevant units) over multiple time periods. This dual dimensionality, the merging of time and entities, bestows panel data with its remarkable analytical prowess.

So, what are the defining characteristics of panel data, and why do we find it so crucial in the realm of econometrics? Let's begin by unpacking its key attributes:

Structure of Panel Data

Imagine a spreadsheet where each row represents a specific entity, while each column corresponds to a particular time point. Each cell within this structure captures data for an entity at a specific moment in time. This data arrangement presents us with rich possibilities for exploration.

Advantages of Panel Data

Panel data is prized in econometrics for several compelling reasons:

Efficient Data Utilization: By observing entities across various time periods, we make the most of our available data. This richer dataset facilitates more robust and comprehensive analyses.

Disentangling Variation: We can tease out the differences and variations in data at the individual entity level, as well as over time. This helps us understand how factors influence change.

Analysis of Dynamic Effects: Panel data enables us to investigate dynamic effects by examining how changes in one variable affect another variable over time.

Capturing Heterogeneity: In a world of diversity, entities often exhibit different characteristics. Panel data allows us to account for and explore these differences, enhancing the accuracy of our analyses.

Now that we appreciate the fundamental structure and advantages of panel data, you might wonder how we make sense of this complex data type. The answer lies in the sophisticated econometric models and techniques that we will explore throughout this chapter.

Our journey through the land of panel data has just begun. In the upcoming sections, we will delve deeper into the econometric models tailor-made for panel data, understand how to handle endogeneity issues, and apply advanced panel data techniques to real-world cases. The empirical research case study towards the end of this chapter will illustrate the practical application of these concepts, cementing your understanding and preparing you to wield panel data as a powerful tool in your econometric arsenal.

Now that we have the map, the compass, and the determination to explore panel data, let's set forth into the realm of econometric analysis, where data reveals its tales, and Python stands as our trusty guide.

Fixed Effects Models

Fixed Effects Models, often referred to as within-effects models, are a cornerstone of panel data analysis. They are particularly useful when we aim to control for unobserved, time-invariant heterogeneity among the entities in our panel.

Picture a dataset that tracks economic variables across multiple countries over several years. Naturally, each country will have inherent differences that remain constant throughout the observation period - factors such as cultural influences, institutional frameworks, or geographical features. Fixed Effects Models allow us to account for and eliminate these unchanging disparities, leaving us with the variance that can be attributed to the variables of interest.

These models are essential for addressing questions like: Does an increase in a country's education expenditure lead to a growth in its GDP per capita over time, considering the diverse underlying characteristics of each nation? Fixed Effects Models help us find answers by removing the influence of these unchanging factors.

Applications of Fixed Effects Models

Fixed Effects Models find extensive applications in economics, sociology, and other fields. They are invaluable when:

Controlling for Unobserved Effects: These models are your best ally when you need to control for factors that remain constant over time and vary across entities, such as firm-specific productivity or individual traits.

Investigating Individual Change: Fixed Effects Models are apt for studying changes within entities over time. For example, you might use them to understand how policies impact the earnings of different workers over several years.

Exploring Policy Effects: In economics, they are widely used to assess the impact of policy changes or interventions. Fixed Effects Models help to isolate the policy's influence from other underlying factors.

Estimating Fixed Effects Models

Python equips us with the means to estimate Fixed Effects Models efficiently. Libraries like StatsModels provide the tools needed to perform this estimation. These models can be estimated using Ordinary Least Squares (OLS) regressions.

Let's dive into a simplified example:

python

import statsmodels.api as sm

Load your panel data

```
data = pd.read_csv('your_data.csv')

# Create dummy variables for each entity
data = pd.get_dummies(data, columns=)

# Define the dependent and independent variables
X = data
y = data

# Create the Fixed Effects model
model = sm.OLS(y, X).fit(cov_type='cluster', cov_kwds={'groups': data})

# Get the summary of the model
print(model.summary())
```

This code snippet highlights the fundamental steps of estimating Fixed Effects Models using Python. The 'entity' dummy variables effectively account for the time-invariant heterogeneity, allowing us to isolate the impact of our independent variable.

Fixed Effects Models serve as our trusty guide to understanding and interpreting data by providing a way to control for unobserved, entity-specific effects. With Python at our side, the path to harnessing this potent econometric tool becomes more accessible than ever.

Random Effects Models

Random Effects Models, also known as mixed-effects models, serve as a powerful tool when dealing with panel data that exhibits both within-entity and between-entity variability. In essence, they enable us to account for unobserved, time-invariant heterogeneity while considering the broader effects that differ between entities in the panel.

Imagine a scenario where you have data on multiple companies over several years, each with its own unique characteristics and internal factors. These unique traits are unchanging over time for each entity but can vary across different entities. Random Effects Models allow us to model this duality, making them particularly suitable for analyzing data with nested structures.

Applications of Random Effects Models

Random Effects Models are versatile and find applications in various fields, from economics to social sciences. They are particularly valuable when:

Accounting for Entity-Specific Characteristics: When you need to analyze data that consists of multiple entities, such as firms, individuals, or countries, and you suspect that entity-specific characteristics influence the dependent variable.

Handling Unobserved Heterogeneity: Random Effects Models allow you to account for unobserved factors that remain constant over time, such as firm-specific productivity or individual traits. This is crucial when you want to estimate the impact of time-varying independent variables while controlling for these unobserved effects.

Capturing Entity-Level Trends: They are effective when you want to capture variations in the dependent variable that are specific to each entity over time.

Estimating Random Effects Models

Python equips us with the tools needed to estimate Random Effects Models efficiently. The StatsModels library, among others, provides the capabilities to perform this estimation. These models can be estimated using the Generalized Least Squares (GLS) method or Maximum Likelihood Estimation (MLE).

Here's a simplified example to get you started:

python

```
import statsmodels.api as sm

# Load your panel data
data = pd.read_csv('your_data.csv')

# Create the Random Effects model
model = sm.MixedLM(data, data, groups=data)
result = model.fit()

# Get the summary of the model
print(result.summary())
```

In this Python example, we employ the MixedLM class from the StatsModels library to estimate the Random Effects Model. The 'entity' variable helps us account for the unobserved heterogeneity among the entities.

Random Effects Models offer a compelling approach to dealing with panel data that combines within-entity and between-entity variability. Python, with its libraries and tools, simplifies the process of estimation and interpretation.

Endogeneity Testing

In the realm of panel data analysis, where we're traversing the intricate landscapes of economic phenomena, understanding and addressing endogeneity issues is pivotal. These issues are like hidden currents beneath the surface, impacting the accuracy of our models. In this section, we'll navigate through what endogeneity is, why it matters, and the methods to test and mitigate its effects.

Unraveling the Enigma of Endogeneity

Endogeneity, a concept deeply rooted in econometrics, refers to the situation where an independent variable in a regression model is correlated with the error term. This correlation violates one of the core assumptions of linear regression: the exogeneity of independent variables.

Picture this: you're examining the relationship between education and income. A common issue is that unobserved variables, like natural ability or motivation, might influence both education levels and income. When these hidden factors affect the independent variable (education), you have endogeneity.

The challenge of endogeneity is that it can lead to biased and inconsistent parameter estimates, rendering your model less reliable and potentially invalidating your findings.

Why Endogeneity Matters

Endogeneity is not just a statistical quirk. It has real-world implications, especially in the field of economics. Let's explore why it matters:

Causality vs. Correlation: When we aim to determine causal relationships, endogeneity can mislead us by showing a mere correlation between variables. This can be problematic, especially when policy decisions or business strategies depend on the results.

Policy Implications: In policy analysis, where we assess the impact of interventions or reforms, endogeneity can distort our estimates. A policy that appears ineffective due to endogeneity might actually be highly impactful when properly addressed.

Investment Decisions: In finance and investment, understanding the drivers of asset prices is crucial. Endogeneity can lead to misguided investment decisions by failing to identify the true drivers of returns.

Testing and Addressing Endogeneity

Now, let's delve into how we can tackle endogeneity:

Instrumental Variables (IV): IV regression is a powerful technique to address endogeneity. It involves finding an instrument, a variable that is correlated with the endogenous variable but not with the error term. IVs help identify causal relationships by removing the correlation between the independent variable and the error term.

python

import statsmodels.api as sm

```python
# Using IV2SLS (Two-Stage Least Squares) for IV regression
iv_model           =           sm.IV2SLS(dependent_variable,
independent_variable, instrument=instrument_variable).fit()
```

Control Functions: Control functions, like the control function approach, can be used when the endogenous variable is a part of a simultaneous equation system. By introducing control functions, we can mitigate the endogeneity bias.

python

```python
control_function  =  control_function(dependent_variable,
independent_variable, control_variables)
```

Differencing: In some cases, differencing the data, whether first-differencing or using fixed effects, can help eliminate endogeneity. This approach is particularly useful when dealing with time-series data.

Granger Causality Test: This test can be used to examine whether one time series can predict another. If one variable Granger-causes another, it may indicate endogeneity.

Panel Data Methods: For panel data, fixed effects models can help mitigate endogeneity by accounting for unobserved time-invariant variables that might be correlated with the endogenous variable.

Endogeneity is a formidable challenge in empirical econometric analysis. By using these methods and techniques, you can detect and address it, ensuring the reliability and validity of your findings. In our journey through Python in econometrics, we equip you with the tools to master these advanced techniques.

Advanced Panel Data Techniques

We've come a long way in our exploration of panel data analysis. By now, you've gained a solid foundation in understanding the power of panel data, delved into fixed and random effects models, and even explored how to tackle the tricky issue of endogeneity. Now, it's time to take a step further into the advanced realm of panel data analysis. This is where the true magic happens, and we'll be discussing two key techniques: dynamic panel data models and selection models.

Dynamic Panel Data Models: Unveiling the Time Dimension

Imagine you have a dataset that not only spans various entities or individuals but also stretches across multiple time periods. This is where dynamic panel data models shine. In this advanced panel data technique, we address the issue of endogeneity that often arises due to unobservable time-invariant variables.

In dynamic models, we introduce lagged values of the dependent variable as independent variables. This helps us control for endogeneity by taking into account the past values of our variables. The inclusion of lagged variables turns our models into systems of equations, making them quite intricate. Nevertheless, these models enable us to better capture the dynamics and dependencies in your data.

Python Example:

python

```python
import statsmodels.api as sm

# Create a dynamic panel data model
dynamic_model = sm.GMM(dependent_variable, independent_variables, time_lagged_variable).fit()
```

Selection Models: Dealing with Sample Selection Bias

In some scenarios, you might find that your dataset doesn't include all the data points you'd ideally want. This is known as sample selection bias. Selection models come to the rescue by addressing this issue.

These models are particularly relevant when your dataset has two parts: the observed part (those included in your dataset) and the unobserved part (those not included). The unobserved part can be critical in understanding the true relationships you're investigating.

Selection models use techniques like Heckman's two-step procedure to account for this bias. By modeling the selection process and estimating the model parameters accordingly, you can obtain more accurate and unbiased results.

Python Example:

python

```python
from statsmodels.survey import selection
```

Create a selection model

selection_model = selection.Probit(endogenous_variable, exogenous_variables, selection_variable).fit()

As we explore these advanced panel data techniques, it's essential to remember that they come with increased complexity. But with the power of Python in your hands, you have the tools to tackle these complexities and uncover valuable insights in your data.

Next, in our journey through Python in econometrics, we will apply these advanced techniques to a real empirical research case in Section 5.6b. This case study will bring together all the knowledge you've gained and demonstrate how to wield these advanced techniques to solve real-world problems.

Join me as we delve into empirical research and discover how these advanced panel data techniques can shape the world of economics and data science.

Empirical Research Case Study

We've navigated through the intricacies of panel data analysis, from understanding the structure and advantages of panel data to exploring fixed and random effects models, addressing the pesky issue of endogeneity, and uncovering advanced panel data techniques. Now, it's time to bring this knowledge to life through a real empirical research case study.

Picture this: You're an economist armed with Python, ready to embark on a journey of discovery. Your mission? To analyze real-world data using the powerful tools and techniques we've explored so far.

The Research Question

Let's set the stage. You've been tasked with assessing the effectiveness of a government policy aimed at reducing unemployment. Your research question is straightforward yet profound: Did the policy lead to a significant decline in unemployment rates? To answer this question, you'll apply what you've learned about panel data analysis.

Data Collection and Preparation

First, you gather the data. Your dataset includes information about employment, wages, and other economic indicators across different regions and time periods. It's a prime example of panel data with a wealth of information waiting to be untangled.

With your data in hand, you dive into the crucial step of data preparation. This is where you'll apply the data cleaning and transformation techniques outlined in Chapter 2.2b and Chapter 2.3b. You'll address missing values, outliers, and perform data imputation where needed.

Modeling the Effects

Now, the real fun begins. You start by setting up your fixed effects and random effects models, a skill you've mastered in Chapter 5.2b and 5.3b. The challenge is to account for the variation both between entities and over time while keeping your eye on the policy's influence.

Once your models are in place, you're ready to dive deep into the data. This is the heart of panel data analysis, and you'll begin with the analysis of the fixed and random effects to tease out valuable insights.

Endogeneity Testing

Endogeneity might rear its head, and it's your job to detect and address it. As you've learned in Chapter 5.4b, panel data offers a unique opportunity to explore the issue of endogeneity. You conduct various tests to determine whether any unobservable variables affect both the policy and unemployment.

Interpreting the Results

The results are in. Your models have been estimated, and the endogeneity tests have been conducted. You uncover fascinating insights into the relationship between the government policy and unemployment rates. It's a moment of truth for your research, and your interpretation skills, honed in Chapter 3.4b, come into play.

Applying the Advanced Techniques

But this case study isn't just about basic panel data analysis. You're here to apply advanced panel data techniques. In this context, dynamic panel data models reveal hidden dynamics that wouldn't be evident in cross-sectional analysis alone. You delve into the complexity of these models, understanding how past values of variables can impact the current employment situation.

Python Example:

python

```
import statsmodels.api as sm

# Create a dynamic panel data model for your research
dynamic_model        =        sm.GMM(dependent_variable,
independent_variables, time_lagged_variable).fit()
```

Drawing Conclusions

As you wrap up the case study, you're not only armed with insightful analysis but also valuable policy recommendations based on the findings. This is where you bridge the gap between data science and economic analysis, connecting your results to real-world decision-making.

The Bigger Picture

This case study illustrates the power of Python in econometrics. By applying the tools and techniques you've learned throughout this book, you've delved deep into a pressing economic issue and come out with a better understanding of its complexities. This is the essence of bridging data science and economic analysis.

In this journey of discovery, Python has been your faithful companion, providing you with the means to analyze, model, and interpret data effectively. As you conclude this chapter, you can take pride in your ability to apply panel data analysis to real-world scenarios, paving the way for more informed policy decisions.

But the story doesn't end here. The next chapter delves into advanced econometric techniques, opening doors to further exploration of economic phenomena. Join me as we venture into the world of instrumental variable regression, limited dependent variable models, and so much more in Chapter 6.

Conclusion

In this chapter, we embarked on a journey into the realm of panel data analysis. From understanding the foundational concepts to delving into advanced panel data techniques, you've acquired a comprehensive skill set for analyzing complex economic data. Our empirical research case study illustrated how these techniques can be applied to answer pressing real-world questions, providing valuable insights into the intricate relationship between government policies and economic outcomes.

As you wrap up this chapter, remember that panel data analysis is a powerful tool for economists, enabling you to extract meaningful information from vast and diverse datasets. The journey doesn't end here; the next chapter takes you into the realm of advanced econometric techniques. Prepare to explore instrumental variable regression, limited dependent variable models, cointegration, and more. These tools will further enhance your capabilities as you continue your quest to bridge data science and economic analysis. Get ready for an exciting dive into the world of econometrics in Chapter 6.

CHAPTER 6: ADVANCED ECONOMETRIC TECHNIQUES

Congratulation on make it to Chapter 6 of "Python in Econometrics: Bridging Data Science and Economic Analysis." In the preceding chapters, you've laid a solid foundation in Python and the fundamental principles of econometrics. Now, it's time to venture into more advanced territories and sharpen your skills in econometric modeling.

In this chapter, we will explore a plethora of advanced econometric techniques that are essential for addressing complex real-world economic problems. These techniques go beyond the basics of linear regression and offer powerful tools to analyze intricate economic relationships, conduct rigorous diagnostics, and make accurate predictions.

Prepare to delve into the world of instrumental variable (IV) regression, limited dependent variable models, cointegration, and error correction models. We will also examine essential model diagnostics and their extensions, allowing you to tackle issues like heteroscedasticity and serial correlation. This chapter offers you a toolkit of advanced methodologies that are indispensable for econometric analysis.

By the end of this chapter, you'll be equipped to address complex econometric problems, conduct sophisticated analyses, and contribute to the field of economic research and policy analysis. Let's take a leap forward into the world of advanced econometric techniques, where your skills will reach new heights and your insights will become even more valuable.

Instrumental Variable (IV) Regression

Instrumental variable (IV) regression is a powerful technique in econometrics that opens doors to addressing some of the most complex challenges in economic analysis. In this section, we will delve into the heart of IV regression, understanding its importance, and gaining the skills needed to estimate IV models effectively.

The Necessity of IV Regression

In traditional linear regression, we make assumptions about the relationships between our independent and dependent variables. We assume that there are no omitted variables or endogeneity issues that might bias our results. However, in the real world, these assumptions often do not hold. Here's where instrumental variable regression comes to the rescue.

IV regression is essential when we encounter endogeneity, a situation where our independent variables are correlated with the error term in our regression model. Such endogeneity can lead to biased and inefficient estimates, rendering our results unreliable. IV regression provides a solution by introducing an exogenous variable, known as the instrumental variable, that is correlated with the potentially endogenous independent variable but not with the error term.

Understanding the Instrumental Variable

The instrumental variable is like a magic wand in econometrics. It allows us to disentangle the complex relationships between variables. This exogenous variable should meet two crucial criteria:

Relevance: The instrumental variable must be correlated with the potentially endogenous variable we aim to study. In other words, it should influence the variable we're interested in.

Exogeneity: The instrumental variable should not be correlated with the error term in our regression model. If it is, it won't serve its purpose as an instrument.

By replacing the endogenous variable with an instrument in our model, we can obtain unbiased and consistent estimates for our parameters. IV regression provides the statistical framework to achieve this, allowing us to isolate the causal relationship we seek to understand.

Estimating IV Models

Now that we understand the importance of instrumental variables let's dive into the process of estimating IV models. This involves a two-stage least squares (2SLS) procedure.

In the first stage, we regress the potentially endogenous variable on the instrumental variable, obtaining a set of fitted values. These fitted values represent the "predicted" values of the endogenous variable based on the instrument.

In the second stage, we replace the potentially endogenous variable in our original model with these fitted values and perform a standard OLS regression. The coefficients we obtain in the second stage represent the causal relationship between our independent and dependent variables.

To illustrate this, let's consider an example involving education and income. We want to understand the impact of education (potentially endogenous) on income. We suspect that unobserved factors, such as motivation, may bias the results. We could use an instrument like the number of years of compulsory education as a proxy for education. This instrument is likely to influence education (relevance) but is unlikely to be correlated with the unobserved factors influencing income (exogeneity).

By conducting a 2SLS regression, we replace education with the predicted values from the first stage (using the instrument) and estimate the relationship between these predicted values and income in the second stage. This helps us obtain an unbiased estimate of the causal effect of education on income.

Real-World Applications

IV regression finds applications in various areas, including economics, social sciences, and public policy. It is used to address endogeneity and omitted variable bias in research on topics like healthcare, education, labor markets, and finance. Furthermore, it plays a significant role in evaluating the impact of policy interventions and economic reforms, where random assignment is not possible.

Instrumental variable regression is a versatile tool in the econometrician's toolkit, allowing us to uncover causal relationships in the midst of complex and intertwined data. In the next sections of this chapter, we will explore even more advanced techniques that build upon this foundation. We'll delve into limited dependent variable models, cointegration, and error correction models, each contributing to a deeper understanding of economic phenomena. So, buckle up and prepare to master the art of advanced econometrics.

Limited Dependent Variable Models

In the intricate world of econometrics, limited dependent variable models play a crucial role in tackling scenarios where the outcome of interest is not continuously distributed. Instead, it falls into distinct categories or exhibits a bounded range. In this section, we will unravel the mysteries of limited dependent variable models, with a particular focus on two fundamental techniques: the logit model and the probit model.

Understanding Limited Dependent Variables

Before we dive into the specifics of these models, let's grasp the concept of limited dependent variables. In many economic and social situations, the outcome we wish to study is not a continuous variable. For instance, when analyzing the decision to purchase a product (yes or no), predicting whether an individual will default on a loan (default or not), or estimating the probability of an event occurring (ranging from 0 to 1), the dependent variable is inherently limited in its range.

Traditional linear regression models, which assume continuous and normally distributed errors, aren't suitable for these situations. Instead, we turn to limited dependent variable models to capture the discrete or bounded nature of the data.

The Logit Model

The logit model, short for logistic regression, is one of the cornerstones of limited dependent variable modeling. It's particularly well-suited for binary outcomes or situations where we're interested in estimating probabilities.

The core idea behind the logit model is to model the log-odds of an event occurring as a linear function of predictor variables. The equation takes the form:

$$\ln\left(\frac{p}{1-p}\right) = \beta_0 + \beta_1 X_1 + \beta_2 X_2 + \ldots + \beta_k X_k$$

Where:

pp represents the probability of the event occurring.

lnln is the natural logarithm.

$\beta_0, \beta_1, \ldots, \beta_k$ are the model parameters.

$X_1, X_2, \ldots, X_k$ are the predictor variables.

The logit model produces results that help us understand the impact of each predictor variable on the odds of the event happening. It's widely used in fields like marketing for predicting consumer behavior, in healthcare for assessing the likelihood of diseases, and in political science for modeling voting choices.

The Probit Model

The probit model is a close relative of the logit model, sharing the goal of modeling binary or limited outcomes. Instead of the log-odds, the probit model models the cumulative standard normal distribution function's inverse, known as the probit function.

The equation for the probit model is quite similar to that of the logit model:

$$\Phi^{-1}(p) = \beta_0 + \beta_1 X_1 + \beta_2 X_2 + \ldots + \beta_k X_k \Phi^{-1}(p) = \beta_0 + \beta_1 X_1 + \beta_2 X_2 + \ldots + \beta_k X_k$$

Where:

$\Phi^{-1}\Phi^{-1}$ represents the probit function.

pp remains the probability of the event occurring.

$\beta_0, \beta_1, \ldots, \beta_k \beta_0, \beta_1, \ldots, \beta_k$ are the model parameters.

$X_1, X_2, \ldots, X_k X_1, X_2, \ldots, X_k$ are the predictor variables.

The results of the probit model are interpreted in a similar manner to the logit model, focusing on how each predictor variable affects the probability of the event. Probit models are commonly used in economics for modeling labor force participation, in psychology for understanding decision-making processes, and in epidemiology for studying disease occurrence.

Applications and Beyond

The applications of logit and probit models are diverse. They extend beyond binary outcomes to scenarios with ordinal dependent variables (more than two categories). These techniques are employed when dealing with questions like predicting credit ratings (poor, fair, good), analyzing customer satisfaction (unsatisfied, neutral, satisfied), or studying preferences for education levels (high school, undergraduate, postgraduate).

In economic research, limited dependent variable models help us tackle intricate questions such as labor force participation, firm decisions, and consumer choices. These models allow us to navigate the nuanced landscape of decision-making, providing valuable insights and predictions.

Cointegration and Error Correction Models

In the previous sections of this book, we've delved into fundamental econometric concepts and regression models. Now, it's time to explore more specialized techniques. In this section, we'll journey into the world of cointegration and error correction models, which are indispensable when dealing with time series data.

Understanding Cointegration

Time series data often exhibit trends and seasonality, making them non-stationary. Traditional regression techniques are typically based on the assumption that the variables are stationary, which means their statistical properties don't change over time. When working with non-stationary data, standard regression can lead to spurious results.

Cointegration is a concept that helps us address this issue. It deals with the integration order of variables, and it plays a vital role when variables have unit roots, implying they are non-stationary. Two or more non-stationary time series are said to be cointegrated if a linear combination of them is stationary.

For instance, consider two variables, A and B, representing the prices of two related commodities. Both A and B might be non-stationary when analyzed individually, but if a linear combination, say A - 2B, results in a stationary series, they are considered cointegrated. This suggests a long-term relationship between A and B, which is crucial in various economic and financial analyses.

Error Correction Models (ECM)

Once we've established cointegration between variables, we can dive into error correction models. These models capture short-term dynamics in variables that are cointegrated. The key idea is that if a long-term relationship exists between variables, then short-term deviations from this equilibrium should be corrected. ECMs are a way to model and understand this process.

In simple terms, an ECM models the relationship between the change in a variable (the first difference) and the difference between its long-term equilibrium and the current value. It involves two components:

The Long-term Relationship: This part represents the cointegration equation. It describes the equilibrium between variables and how they interact over the long term. For example, in our commodities example, it might express how changes in the price of A and B are related in the long run.

The Short-term Dynamics: The error correction term accounts for short-term deviations from the equilibrium. It shows how quickly variables adjust to their long-term relationship when they move apart. This term is usually represented by a coefficient, which tells us about the speed of adjustment.

Applications in Time Series Data

Cointegration and error correction models find numerous applications in economics and finance. Let's look at a few examples:

Interest Rate Parity: Cointegration is used to analyze the relationship between interest rates in different countries. It helps us understand how exchange rates adjust in the short run to maintain parity with interest rates, as well as deviations from this parity.

Stock Prices and Dividends: Analysts use cointegration and ECMs to model the relationship between stock prices and dividends. This is crucial in understanding how quickly stock prices adjust to changes in dividend payments.

Purchasing Power Parity: In international economics, the theory of purchasing power parity suggests that exchange rates should adjust to equalize the prices of identical goods in any two countries. Cointegration helps examine the validity of this theory.

Macroeconomic Variables: Economists use these techniques to analyze the relationships between macroeconomic variables such as GDP, consumption, and investment. This helps in understanding the dynamics of economic systems.

Now, it's time for a Python touch. When dealing with cointegration and ECMs in Python, you'll often work with libraries like StatsModels. Here's a simplified example:

```python
python

import statsmodels.api as sm
import pandas as pd

# Assuming 'data' is your DataFrame with time series variables
model = sm.OLS(data, data)
results = model.fit()

# Check for cointegration
cointegration_test = sm.tsa.adfuller(results.resid)

# If cointegrated, proceed with ECM modeling
```

In this example, we're using StatsModels to perform cointegration tests and analyze the relationship between two variables, A and B. This Python snippet helps you take your theoretical understanding and put it into practice.

Cointegration and error correction models are powerful tools when dealing with non-stationary time series data. They allow us to uncover long-term relationships and understand how variables correct themselves in the short run. By applying these concepts in Python, you can harness their potential for economic and financial analysis. So, prepare to explore these techniques further and apply them to real-world scenarios as we proceed through this chapter.

Model Diagnostics and Extensions

In our journey through Python in econometrics, we've learned about various advanced econometric techniques, from instrumental variable (IV) regression to limited dependent variable models. Now, as we delve deeper into the intricacies of econometric analysis, we arrive at the critical stage of model diagnostics and extensions. In this chapter section, we explore the essential elements of model diagnostics, focusing on two significant aspects: heteroscedasticity and serial correlation tests. These diagnostic tools serve as the guiding lights to ensure the robustness and reliability of our econometric models.

Heteroscedasticity: Understanding Variance Disparities

Heteroscedasticity, a mouthful of a term, is a fundamental issue in econometrics. It refers to the situation where the variance of errors in a regression model is not constant across all values of the independent variables. In simple terms, it means that the spread of residuals (the differences between observed and predicted values) varies as you move along the range of the predictors.

Why is this a problem? Well, it can lead to biased and inefficient parameter estimates, affecting the validity of your model. It could also give a false impression of statistical significance. To tackle this issue, we employ diagnostic tests like the Breusch-

Pagan and White tests, both of which are available in Python libraries like statsmodels.

To apply these tests, you need to understand the underlying principle. The null hypothesis for both tests assumes homoscedasticity, meaning constant variance. If the p-value associated with the test is small (typically below 0.05), you can reject this null hypothesis, suggesting the presence of heteroscedasticity. In such a scenario, you may consider transformations or robust standard errors to address the issue.

Now, let's see a Python example of how to perform these tests and deal with heteroscedasticity.

python

```
import statsmodels.api as sm

from statsmodels.compat import lzip

from statsmodels.stats.diagnostic import het_breuschpagan, het_white

# Fit your regression model
model = sm.OLS(y, X).fit()

# Apply Breusch-Pagan test
bp_test = het_breuschpagan(model.resid, model.model.exog)
lzip(, bp_test)

# Apply White test
white_test = het_white(model.resid, model.model.exog)
lzip(, white_test)
```

Serial Correlation: Dealing with Auto-correlation

Serial correlation, often known as autocorrelation, is another concern in econometrics, particularly in time series analysis. It arises when the residuals of a model are correlated with each other. In simpler terms, it means that the error terms at one time point are dependent on the errors at a previous time point. This can violate the assumption of independent errors, potentially rendering our parameter estimates inefficient and biased.

To detect serial correlation, we employ tests like the Durbin-Watson test and the Ljung-Box test. If these tests indicate the presence of serial correlation, it's essential to address the issue. In time series data, this is typically achieved through differencing or including lagged values of the dependent variable in the model.

Now, let's take a look at how to apply these tests in Python:

python

```
from statsmodels.stats.stattools import durbin_watson
from statsmodels.stats.diagnostic import acorr_ljungbox

# Calculate Durbin-Watson statistic
durbin_watson_stat = durbin_watson(model.resid)

# Perform the Ljung-Box test for serial correlation
lb_test_stat, lb_p_value = acorr_ljungbox(model.resid)
```

We've explored the critical aspects of model diagnostics,

focusing on heteroscedasticity and serial correlation tests. By mastering these tools and applying them correctly, you can ensure the validity and reliability of your econometric models. So, as we move forward in this journey, keep these diagnostics close at hand, ensuring the robustness of your analyses. In the world of econometrics, the devil is often in the details, and it's these details that make all the difference.

Understanding the Power of IV Regression

Before we jump into policy impact assessment, let's quickly revisit why instrumental variable regression is so essential. IV regression is a statistical technique used when there's a concern about endogeneity, where the independent variable in a standard regression model is correlated with the error term. In such cases, ordinary least squares (OLS) estimates may be biased and inconsistent.

IV regression allows us to tackle this issue by finding an instrumental variable, a variable that is highly correlated with the endogenous variable but not directly correlated with the error term. This instrument helps us identify a causal relationship between the independent variable and the dependent variable. It's a critical technique for assessing the effects of policies or interventions, where endogeneity is a common concern.

Setting the Stage with Python Code

Let's start by setting the stage with some Python code that demonstrates how to conduct an IV regression for policy impact assessment. For this example, imagine we're assessing the impact of a new education policy on economic growth. We suspect endogeneity because regions with better economic growth might invest more in education. Our instrumental variable will be a historical education index that is theoretically related to education investments but not directly influenced by current economic growth.

Here's a simplified Python code example:

python

```
import statsmodels.api as sm
import numpy as np

# Simulated data for policy impact assessment
np.random.seed(0)
n = 1000

# Simulate the endogenous variable (education investment)
education_investment = np.random.normal(10, 2, n)

# Simulate the dependent variable (economic growth)
economic_growth = 2 + 0.5 * education_investment + np.random.normal(0, 1, n)

# Simulate the instrumental variable (historical education index)
historical_education = np.random.normal(8, 2, n)

# Perform the IV regression
iv_regression = sm.OLS(economic_growth, sm.add_constant(education_investment)).fit()
iv_results =
```

```
iv_regression.get_robustcov_results(cov_type='HC3')

# Instrumental variable regression summary
print(iv_results.summary())
```

This code showcases a basic IV regression setup using Python's StatsModels library. We generate simulated data for education investment, economic growth, and the instrumental variable (historical education index). Then, we perform the IV regression to assess the impact of education investment on economic growth while addressing endogeneity.

Policy Impact Assessment in the Real World

In practice, the applications of IV regression for policy impact assessment can be much more complex. We often deal with a myriad of variables and datasets to evaluate the effects of policies or interventions, ranging from healthcare reforms to economic stimulus packages.

Consider a real-world example where an economic policy aims to reduce unemployment rates. To assess its impact, you would need data on the policy implementation, employment rates, and a credible instrumental variable. Once you have these components, you can follow a similar Python coding structure to evaluate the policy's effectiveness.

Conclusion: Leveraging Python for Informed Policy Decisions

In this section, we've explored how instrumental variable regression can be a powerful tool for assessing the impact of policies and interventions. By employing Python and the IV regression technique, you can untangle the complexities of endogeneity and provide valuable insights for informed policy decisions. As you embark on your journey through the realm of econometrics, remember that the ability to rigorously evaluate the effects of policies is a skill with wide-reaching implications, making you an invaluable asset in the field of economics.

Real-world Application and Case Study

We've examined advanced econometric techniques, honing our skills and knowledge. Now, it's time to bridge the theoretical world of Python in econometrics with the practical realm. In this section, we'll put our expertise to the test by applying advanced econometric techniques to a real-world case study.

Why Real-world Application Matters

As we journey through this book, the focus has been on learning the theoretical underpinnings of econometrics and mastering the tools Python provides. But all this knowledge gains its true value when it's put into practice in real-world scenarios.

Econometrics isn't just an academic exercise. It's a powerful tool for economists to analyze, understand, and influence the world around them. By applying econometric techniques to actual data, we can uncover insights, make informed decisions, and provide solutions to real economic problems.

The Case Study: Unraveling the Housing Market

For our case study, let's immerse ourselves in a common yet multifaceted issue - the housing market. Housing markets are of utmost significance in any economy, with implications spanning from the personal finances of individuals to the broader economic stability of a nation.

Imagine that you're tasked with analyzing the factors affecting housing prices in a particular city over the past decade. Your goal is to understand how variables like interest rates, population growth, and economic conditions impact housing prices. This information is crucial for potential buyers, real estate investors, and policymakers.

Python in Action

Python is our trusty companion in this endeavor. We'll harness its formidable capabilities to analyze and interpret the data, using a blend of regression models, time series analysis, and other advanced econometric techniques. Python's versatile libraries, such as NumPy, pandas, and StatsModels, will prove indispensable.

Let's delve into a snippet of Python code to give you a taste of what's involved:

```python
import pandas as pd
import statsmodels.api as sm
```

```
# Load the dataset
housing_data = pd.read_csv('housing_data.csv')

# Perform multiple regression to understand the factors
affecting housing prices
X = housing_data
X = sm.add_constant(X) # Add a constant for the intercept
y = housing_data

model = sm.OLS(y, X).fit()

# Print the regression summary
print(model.summary())
```

In this code, we load a dataset containing information on interest rates, population growth, economic conditions, and housing prices. We then perform a multiple regression analysis to unveil the relationships between these variables. Python's StatsModels library is a valuable ally in this journey, providing detailed insights into the regression results.

Interpreting the Results

Once we run the regression, we can interpret the results to draw meaningful conclusions. What factors have the most significant impact on housing prices? Are there interactions or unexpected relationships?

This real-world application allows us to not only apply Python in econometrics but also understand the practical challenges and intricacies of analyzing data and making informed decisions.

Conclusion: Applying Knowledge to Influence the World

In this chapter, we've ventured beyond theory, diving into the practical world of applying advanced econometric techniques to real scenarios. We've harnessed the power of Python to analyze data and derive valuable insights. The case study on housing prices demonstrates the significance of these techniques in solving complex economic puzzles.

As we wrap up this chapter, you've witnessed the transformation of knowledge into actionable skills. But our journey doesn't end here. In the next chapter, we'll embark on a new exploration - "Machine Learning for Econometrics." Get ready to unlock the potential of machine learning in understanding and predicting economic trends. Join us as we delve deeper into the intersection of data science and economic analysis, taking your skills to new heights.

CHAPTER 7: MACHINE LEARNING FOR ECONOMETRICS

Welcome to the chapter you've been waiting for, where things getting really interesting, In our journey to bridge data science and economic analysis using Python, we've covered fundamental econometric techniques. Now, we take a bold step into the world of machine learning—a realm of endless possibilities for economists.

Machine learning offers a new dimension to econometric analysis, allowing us to harness the power of algorithms and data-driven insights. In this chapter, we'll explore how machine learning techniques, both supervised and unsupervised, can revolutionize the way we analyze and predict economic phenomena.

Get ready to delve into linear regression, decision trees, ensemble methods, clustering, and dimensionality reduction. We'll also address vital topics like model evaluation, hyperparameter tuning, and ethical considerations in the context of econometrics. The culmination of this chapter, the economic prediction case study, will reveal how machine learning can be a game-changer in forecasting economic trends.

In the ever-evolving landscape of economics, data-driven insights have become paramount. It's not enough to rely solely on traditional econometric methods; we must harness the power of machine learning to unlock the hidden patterns and trends within economic data. Welcome to the world of machine learning for econometrics.

The Marriage of Machine Learning and Economics

Machine learning offers economists a transformative toolkit, allowing us to explore and exploit the massive volumes of data at our disposal. But what is machine learning, and how does it relate to econometrics?

At its core, machine learning is a subfield of artificial intelligence that focuses on the development of algorithms and statistical models. These algorithms enable systems to learn and make predictions or decisions without being explicitly programmed. In the realm of economics, machine learning is a game-changer, offering advanced techniques to analyze complex economic phenomena.

The Role of Machine Learning in Econometrics

Machine learning plays a pivotal role in econometrics by facilitating a data-driven approach to economic analysis. In this chapter, we'll delve into two primary branches of machine learning: supervised and unsupervised learning.

Supervised Learning: Guided Insights

Supervised learning is like having a knowledgeable guide through the wilderness of economic data. In this approach, we feed the algorithm with labeled data, allowing it to learn the underlying patterns. Once trained, the model can make predictions or classifications on new, unseen data.

Consider supervised learning as your trusty compass in the economic landscape. It enables us to perform tasks like forecasting GDP growth, predicting stock prices, or classifying economic events. Within this category, we will explore linear regression, decision trees, and ensemble methods.

Linear Regression: Linear regression helps us understand the relationships between economic variables by fitting a linear model to the data. We'll delve into its formula and interpretation, unveiling its potential in predicting economic trends.

Decision Trees: Decision trees are like a roadmap through the maze of economic decision-making. We'll discuss how these trees work, their strengths, and how they can be applied to economic scenarios.

Ensemble Methods: Just as an ensemble cast makes a movie greater than the sum of its parts, ensemble methods combine various models for enhanced accuracy. We'll explore how ensembles can improve economic predictions and decision-making.

Unsupervised Learning: Discovering Hidden Patterns

Unsupervised learning, on the other hand, is like embarking on an uncharted expedition through the economic wilderness. Here, the algorithm explores unlabeled data to identify hidden structures, patterns, or relationships.

Within unsupervised learning, we will delve into clustering and dimensionality reduction techniques.

Clustering: Clustering is akin to grouping similar economic entities together. We'll explore how this technique can be used for market segmentation, identifying economic clusters, or understanding consumer behavior.

Dimensionality Reduction: In the vast ocean of economic data, dimensionality reduction techniques help us navigate efficiently. We'll uncover methods that allow us to simplify complex data while preserving critical information.

Our Exploration Awaits

Our journey into the world of machine learning in econometrics is just beginning. In the upcoming sections, we'll discuss the practical aspects of implementing these machine learning techniques, including model evaluation and hyperparameter tuning.

We'll also address ethical considerations—critical in today's data-driven world. Understanding the potential for bias and fairness issues in machine learning applications is vital for responsible economic analysis.

Supervised Learning

As we delve into the realm of machine learning within the field of econometrics, we encounter one of its most essential branches: supervised learning. Imagine it as a guiding hand through the intricate web of economic data, helping us make predictions, solve problems, and make informed decisions.

In this section, we will explore the fundamental supervised learning techniques and how they can be harnessed to enhance our understanding of economic phenomena.

Linear Regression: Deciphering Economic Relationships

Let's start our journey with one of the most recognizable and intuitive techniques: linear regression. It's like the compass of the econometric world, providing direction by uncovering the relationships between economic variables. Linear regression models are a staple in economic analysis, allowing us to quantify and interpret these relationships.

At its core, linear regression seeks to find the best-fitting straight line (hence "linear") through the data points. This line represents the relationship between a dependent variable (usually the one we want to predict) and one or more independent variables. The equation of this line allows us to predict the value of the dependent variable based on the values of the independent variables.

For instance, in economics, you might use linear regression to determine the influence of factors like inflation, interest rates, and unemployment on economic growth. By analyzing historical data, a linear regression model can reveal the strength and nature of these relationships.

Decision Trees: Navigating Economic Decision-Making

Now, picture decision trees as your map through the intricate forest of economic choices. These models are incredibly versatile and can guide us through complex decision-making processes. Decision trees allow us to visualize potential decisions and their consequences.

A decision tree consists of nodes, branches, and leaves. Each node represents a decision or a test on an attribute, each branch represents an outcome of that decision, and each leaf node represents a decision or a prediction.

In economics, decision trees can be used for various purposes. For example, in financial risk assessment, they can help identify potential risk factors and their impact on investment decisions. Decision trees are excellent tools for both prediction and classification tasks, making them invaluable for economic analysts.

Ensemble Methods: The Power of Teamwork

While decision trees are valuable on their own, we can take our analysis to the next level with ensemble methods. Think of ensemble methods as the Avengers of machine learning. They bring together different models to form a formidable team, enhancing prediction accuracy and robustness.

Ensemble methods combine the predictions from multiple models, which can be decision trees or other base models, to make more accurate and reliable predictions. This approach is particularly helpful in cases where a single model may not capture the complexity of economic data effectively.

For example, in stock market prediction, you can employ ensemble methods to create a portfolio of models that collectively make more accurate predictions about the future price of stocks. The diversity of these models and their combined strength can help you make more informed investment decisions.

Connecting the Dots

Now that we've introduced these fundamental supervised learning techniques, you might be wondering how to apply them in Python. The beauty of Python lies in its extensive libraries for machine learning. Libraries like scikit-learn provide a -friendly interface to implement these techniques with ease.

For instance, in Python, you can perform linear regression using scikit-learn's LinearRegression class. To build a decision tree model, scikit-learn offers DecisionTreeRegressor for regression problems and DecisionTreeClassifier for classification tasks. When it comes to ensemble methods, you can explore the RandomForestRegressor or RandomForestClassifier, which utilize multiple decision trees.

In the subsequent sections of this chapter, we'll dive into practical applications and hands-on examples of implementing these supervised learning techniques. You'll witness how Python's simplicity and power converge to empower economists to make data-driven predictions and informed decisions.

In the world of economics, where countless variables and uncertainties come into play, supervised learning techniques act as our trusty companions. With linear regression, decision trees, and ensemble methods by our side, we can dissect intricate relationships, navigate complex decisions, and harness the collective power of machine learning.

So, fasten your seatbelts, and let's embark on this journey of applying supervised learning techniques to real-world economic data. As we continue, you'll gain the skills and knowledge needed to tackle economic challenges with data-driven solutions. Welcome to the world of machine learning in econometrics, where the power of Python meets the complexity of economics.

Unsupervised Learning

In the vast realm of machine learning, unsupervised learning is akin to a puzzle waiting to be solved. It's the art of finding patterns and structures within data without the guidance of labeled outcomes, a bit like a treasure hunt where the map is concealed within the data itself. In this section, we delve into the world of unsupervised learning, particularly focusing on clustering and dimensionality reduction.

Uncovering Hidden Patterns with Clustering

Clustering is a fascinating concept where the objective is to group similar data points together. Think of it as organizing a vast collection of books into distinct genres without any prior knowledge of the titles. In economics, this technique can help us detect segments within a market, identify customer behavior patterns, or understand economic clusters within regions.

One common method of clustering is the K-means algorithm. It's like an explorer dividing a treasure map into clusters where each group is more likely to contain valuable information. K-means partitions data into K clusters, with each cluster having data points that are closer to each other in terms of similarity. Python offers powerful libraries such as scikit-learn to apply the K-means algorithm effortlessly.

Reducing Complexity with Dimensionality Reduction

Economic data often comes in high dimensions, much like

exploring a multi-dimensional treasure map. Dimensionality reduction techniques are like deciphering the map to reveal the most essential features. By reducing the number of variables, we simplify the problem while retaining the core information.

Principal Component Analysis (PCA) is a widely used dimensionality reduction technique. It's akin to transforming our treasure map into a simpler, 2D version. PCA identifies the most critical dimensions (principal components) that capture the most variation in the data. In economic analysis, this can help us understand which variables influence economic phenomena the most.

Connecting the Dots with Python

Implementing unsupervised learning techniques in Python is surprisingly straightforward, thanks to libraries like scikit-learn and NumPy. You can quickly employ these techniques to extract valuable insights from economic data.

For example, to apply K-means clustering in Python, you can use scikit-learn's KMeans class. This allows you to specify the number of clusters and find groupings within your economic data. Visualizing these clusters can offer profound insights into economic behaviors and trends.

On the other hand, PCA can be seamlessly executed using the PCA class from scikit-learn. This technique reduces the dimensions of your data, making it more manageable while preserving the essence of the information. You'll be amazed at how this can simplify the interpretation of complex economic phenomena.

The Road Ahead

As we journey through the world of unsupervised learning, you'll uncover the beauty of discovering hidden patterns and simplifying complex economic data. Clustering and dimensionality reduction are your tools to reveal the treasure troves of insights concealed within your datasets.

In the subsequent sections of this chapter, we will dive into practical examples and case studies, demonstrating how Python and machine learning can be harnessed to solve real-world economic problems using these unsupervised learning techniques. You'll be equipped with the knowledge and skills to harness the power of unsupervised learning to extract valuable economic insights.

So, get ready to embark on an exciting adventure of unsupervised learning in econometrics. With Python as your trusty companion and the techniques of clustering and dimensionality reduction at your disposal, you're well-prepared to navigate the intricate world of economic data analysis. As we delve into real-world examples and applications, you'll witness firsthand the transformative potential of these methods in economic analysis.

Model Evaluation and Hyperparameter Tuning

In our discovery of machine learning for econometrics, we've explored how to build predictive models, handle data, and apply various algorithms. Now, we reach a crucial juncture where we evaluate these models' performance and fine-tune them for optimal results. Welcome to the realm of model evaluation and hyperparameter tuning.

Measuring Success: Model Evaluation Metrics

Before we dive into the technicalities of model evaluation, let's establish a fundamental concept: how do we know if a model is good? In the context of machine learning, the answer lies in model evaluation metrics. These metrics provide us with a yardstick to measure the performance of our models.

One common metric for regression tasks is the Mean Squared Error (MSE). It quantifies how well our model's predictions align with the actual values. The lower the MSE, the better our model's performance. In Python, we can effortlessly compute the MSE using libraries like scikit-learn.

For classification problems, we often employ metrics like accuracy, precision, recall, and F1-score. These metrics enable us to assess how well our model classifies data correctly. Evaluating these metrics allows us to make informed decisions about model effectiveness.

The Power of Cross-Validation

As we venture deeper into the evaluation process, we encounter the concept of cross-validation. Think of it as stress-testing your model. Cross-validation involves splitting your data into multiple subsets or "folds" and systematically training and testing the model on different combinations. This process ensures that your model generalizes well to unseen data.

One popular cross-validation technique is k-fold cross-validation, where you divide your data into k subsets, train the model on k-1 of them, and test on the remaining one. This process is repeated k times, ensuring that every data point is part of the test set exactly once. Scikit-learn offers efficient tools to implement cross-validation effortlessly.

Fine-Tuning the Model: Hyperparameter Optimization

Machine learning models often come with parameters that you can adjust to optimize their performance. These parameters are known as hyperparameters, and hyperparameter tuning is the process of finding the best combination of values for them.

Grid search and random search are two common techniques for hyperparameter tuning. Grid search involves specifying a set of hyperparameters and their possible values, and the technique explores all combinations systematically. Random search, on the other hand, randomly samples combinations, which can be more efficient in some cases.

In Python, libraries like scikit-learn provide functionalities to implement these techniques. You can systematically search through hyperparameter combinations to find the configuration that yields the best results for your model.

Putting Theory into Practice with Python

Let's put theory into practice with a Python example. Suppose you've built a machine learning model to predict economic trends based on historical data. To evaluate its performance, you calculate metrics such as MSE, accuracy, precision, recall, and F1-score. The model's performance is assessed not just on a single set of data but through k-fold cross-validation, ensuring robustness.

You've also ventured into the world of hyperparameter tuning. Using grid search or random search, you fine-tune your model to achieve the best results. For instance, you might adjust hyperparameters related to the model's learning rate, the depth of decision trees, or the number of hidden layers in a neural network.

By the end of this section, you'll be equipped with a comprehensive understanding of how to evaluate machine learning models and optimize them through hyperparameter tuning. These skills are essential for building reliable models in econometrics, where accuracy and precision matter greatly.

The road ahead in our exploration of machine learning for econometrics is paved with exciting challenges and real-world applications. In the next section, we'll delve into a fascinating case study where we use machine learning to predict economic trends or events, applying the knowledge you've gained about model evaluation and hyperparameter tuning. Get ready to witness the power of Python in econometrics once again.

Economic Prediction Case Study

So far we've explored the intersection of Python, econometrics, and the vast landscape of machine learning. As we delve deeper into this realm, it's time to put our newfound knowledge to the test. In this section, we step into the practical world of economic prediction through a captivating case study.

The Power of Machine Learning in Economics

Machine learning has transformed the way we analyze economic data and make predictions. It empowers us to uncover intricate patterns and relationships within economic variables, enabling us to anticipate economic trends and events with a remarkable level of accuracy. To illustrate the potential of this synergy, we present an engaging economic prediction case study.

Defining the Problem

Imagine a scenario where you're tasked with predicting the stock market's performance. This is a classic example of an economic prediction problem, and it's one of the most widely analyzed subjects in finance and economics. Economic events, policy changes, and global market dynamics all contribute to the complex fluctuations in stock prices. Using machine learning, we aim to build a predictive model that can help investors and policymakers make informed decisions.

The Data

Our journey begins with data. In the world of finance and economics, historical data is a treasure trove. It contains information about stock prices, trading volumes, economic indicators, and other relevant variables. Python offers a wide array of libraries for data retrieval and manipulation, such as pandas, which we've already explored in the Data Preparation chapter.

Once we've gathered our data, we can start the process of feature engineering. This involves selecting relevant variables, creating new features, and ensuring that our dataset is well-prepared for the machine learning model. In the context of stock market prediction, these features could include moving averages, trading volumes, and even macroeconomic indicators like GDP growth.

Choosing the Right Algorithm

Machine learning provides us with a rich toolbox of algorithms, each suited to different types of problems. For time series prediction like stock prices, recurrent neural networks (RNNs) and long short-term memory networks (LSTMs) are often used due to their ability to capture sequential dependencies. Regression algorithms like linear regression can also be applied.

Our Python code would include selecting the appropriate algorithm, splitting the data into training and testing sets, and training the model on historical data. We would then test the model's performance on unseen data to ensure it can generalize well.

Evaluating Model Performance

Model evaluation is a critical step in any machine learning project. For our economic prediction model, we would use appropriate metrics to assess its accuracy and reliability. Common metrics include Mean Absolute Error (MAE), Mean Squared Error (MSE), and Root Mean Squared Error (RMSE) for regression tasks. These metrics quantify the difference between the predicted stock prices and the actual prices.

Cross-validation would play a crucial role here, ensuring that our model performs consistently across different time periods. The K-fold cross-validation technique, which we've discussed earlier in the book, can be particularly useful.

Real-World Application

Once we have a well-validated model, it's time to apply it to real-world data. In our economic prediction case study, we'd feed the model with the latest economic and financial data to generate predictions about future stock prices. This information is invaluable for investors, financial analysts, and policymakers looking to make data-driven decisions.

The Power and Responsibility of Machine Learning

Machine learning is a remarkable tool, capable of unveiling intricate patterns, making predictions, and automating decision-making processes. However, it's imperative to recognize that with great power comes great responsibility. In the field of econometrics, where data drives economic and policy decisions, ethical considerations are not just an afterthought but a fundamental aspect of the entire process.

The Challenge of Bias and Fairness

One of the most critical ethical considerations in machine learning is the issue of bias. Machine learning models learn from historical data, and if that data contains biases, these biases can be perpetuated and even amplified in the predictions they make. In econometrics, where decisions can impact people's livelihoods, unbiased and fair predictions are paramount.

Consider, for instance, a model used to predict loan approvals. If historical data shows a bias against certain groups, such as racial or gender biases, it can lead to unfair denials of loans to individuals in these groups. This not only has ethical implications but can also lead to legal consequences and financial disparities.

Addressing Bias in Machine Learning

In Python, we have a range of tools at our disposal to address bias and fairness in machine learning models. Libraries like scikit-learn provide functionalities to detect and mitigate bias in datasets. For instance, re-sampling techniques, such as oversampling underrepresented groups or undersampling overrepresented groups, can be employed to create a balanced dataset.

Moreover, fairness metrics can be defined and optimized during model training. These metrics assess the fairness of model predictions across different demographic groups, helping to ensure that no particular group is disproportionately affected.

Transparency and Explainability

Another key aspect of ethical machine learning in econometrics is transparency and explainability. It's crucial that the decisions made by machine learning models are understandable and interpretable. Complex models like neural networks may provide high accuracy, but they often lack transparency.

In Python, we can employ techniques to interpret models, such as generating feature importance plots or utilizing model-agnostic interpretability tools. This ensures that end-s, whether they are policymakers, economists, or data scientists, can comprehend the reasons behind the model's predictions.

The Ongoing Dialogue

Ethical considerations in machine learning and econometrics are a subject of ongoing dialogue and debate. As we delve into these ethical dimensions, it's essential to stay updated with the latest developments in the field. Whether it's emerging regulations, guidelines, or best practices, keeping an ear to the ground is a must.

Python, with its rich ecosystem of libraries, facilitates this ongoing dialogue. You can use it to implement evolving fairness metrics, stay compliant with emerging regulations, and embrace best practices for transparent and ethical AI.

The Broader Impact of Ethical Machine Learning

Ethical considerations in machine learning extend beyond individual models. They have the power to shape broader societal and economic outcomes. Ethical AI in econometrics ensures that data-driven decisions align with the values of fairness, equity, and justice. This, in turn, contributes to healthier economies and more equitable societies.

As we approach the conclusion of this section on ethical considerations, we underscore the imperative of maintaining a principled approach throughout the econometric analysis. It's not just about producing accurate predictions; it's about making the world a better place by doing so.

In the next section, we navigate through the fascinating world of economic modeling and simulations, discovering how Python equips us to model economic scenarios and assess policy impacts. It's a journey through hypothetical worlds that have real-world implications.

Conclusion

In the realm of Python, machine learning, and econometrics, We've explored the powerful role machine learning plays in econometrics, from simple linear regressions to complex models. Our path led us through the diverse terrain of supervised and unsupervised learning, where we unraveled the mysteries of linear regression, decision trees, and clustering, among others.

Yet, no exploration of machine learning is complete without contemplating the ethical considerations that underpin every model, prediction, and decision. Our journey through ethical AI reinforced the crucial responsibility we hold to mitigate bias, ensure fairness, and enhance transparency in our models. This ethical compass guides us in an era where data shapes economies and influences policies.

As we conclude our voyage through Chapter 7, we emphasize that the fusion of machine learning with econometrics is not a mere academic exercise. It has real-world applications with far-reaching consequences, affecting economic decisions, policy formulations, and societal well-being. It's a harmonious blend of data science and economic analysis that demands precision, responsibility, and foresight.

Our expedition through the chapters of this book has equipped us with the knowledge, skills, and tools to navigate the complex waters where Python and econometrics meet. But the journey doesn't end here; it's merely a waypoint on a path of continuous learning and discovery.

In the chapters that follow, we delve into economic modeling, data visualization, best practices, and beyond. Our quest for mastering Python in econometrics continues, and the horizons are boundless. Join us as we move forward, equipped with the expertise and wisdom gained so far, ready to unravel the mysteries that lie ahead.

CHAPTER 8: ECONOMIC MODELING AND SIMULATIONS

As we embark on the eighth chapter of "Python in Econometrics: Bridging Data Science and Economic Analysis," we find ourselves standing at the threshold of a fascinating domain. Economic modeling and simulations represent the art of translating complex economic systems into mathematical equations and running scenarios to understand their behavior. This chapter bridges the gap between abstract economic concepts and tangible, data-driven insights, showing how Python can be a potent tool for modeling, simulating, and understanding the economic world.

Economic models are the compasses guiding policymakers, researchers, and analysts through the labyrinth of economic decisions. With Python at our side, we have the power to create, analyze, and simulate these models, transforming theoretical concepts into practical tools for forecasting, policy analysis, and decision-making.

In this chapter, we will venture into the intricate art of building economic models. We'll explore the methods and techniques used to specify equations, define parameters, and bring these models to life through simulations. We'll decipher the results of these simulations to gain a deeper understanding of how policies, economic changes, and external shocks affect our complex economic landscapes.

As we progress through Chapter 8, we will explore the nuanced aspects of economic modeling, from specifying equations to understanding simulation results. You'll be equipped with the knowledge and skills to simulate the impact of policy changes, analyze the outcomes, and make well-informed decisions based on your economic models.

This chapter is a gateway to demystifying economic dynamics using Python. Whether you're a seasoned economist or a data scientist diving into the world of economics, Chapter 8 holds invaluable insights and techniques for you. Together, we'll navigate the intricate world of economic modeling and simulations, uncovering the profound influence these tools have on shaping economic policies and strategies.

Building Economic Models

Economic models are the heart of economic analysis, where Python becomes a masterful tool for crafting models that unravel the intricate tapestry of our economic world. In this chapter, we will delve into the art of building economic models with Python, demystifying the process and providing you with the knowledge to create models that mirror economic reality.

Economic models are the bedrock of economic analysis. They allow us to represent complex systems, identify key relationships, and predict the impact of various factors. But how do we construct these models using Python?

To begin, let's consider the fundamental building blocks of an economic model: equations and parameters. In Python, equations are the mathematical relationships that describe how economic variables interact. These equations capture cause-and-effect relationships, such as supply and demand or production functions.

Parameters, on the other hand, are the constants or coefficients within these equations that determine the strength and direction of the relationships. They represent real-world values, like price elasticities or technology coefficients, that are crucial for the model's accuracy.

The process of building economic models involves the following key steps:

Problem Formulation: The first step is to clearly define the economic problem you aim to solve. What are the key variables and relationships that govern this problem? For instance, if you're modeling supply and demand for a particular product, you'll need to identify variables like price, quantity, and consumer preferences.

Equation Specification: Once the problem is well-defined, you'll proceed to specify the mathematical equations that represent the relationships among these variables. Equations can be simple or complex, linear or nonlinear, depending on the economic phenomena you're modeling.

python

```
# Example: Simple Linear Demand Equation
demand = a - b * price
```

Here, 'demand' is the quantity demanded, 'a' and 'b' are parameters, and 'price' is the product's price.

Parameter Estimation: Parameters are estimated using various techniques, including econometric methods. Python provides a range of libraries like NumPy and SciPy to perform parameter estimation.

python

```
# Example: Estimating 'a' and 'b' using OLS (Ordinary Least Squares) regression
import numpy as np
from scipy.optimize import curve_fit

def linear_demand(price, a, b):
    return a - b * price

popt, _ = curve_fit(linear_demand, prices, quantities)
a, b = popt
```

Model Validation: Validating your model is essential to ensure it accurately reflects real-world economic behavior. This can involve comparing model predictions with observed data or conducting goodness-of-fit tests.

Sensitivity Analysis: Economic models are often subject to uncertainties in parameter values. Sensitivity analysis helps assess how variations in these parameters affect model outcomes. Python's libraries, like Matplotlib, can aid in visualizing sensitivity.

Once you've crafted your economic model in Python, you possess a tool that can provide valuable insights. You can perform "what-if" analyses to understand how changes in variables or policies affect economic outcomes. Moreover, simulations allow you to explore different scenarios, making informed decisions based on the model's predictions.

In the world of economic modeling, Python offers a rich ecosystem of libraries to assist you. Whether you're dealing with intricate simultaneous equations, agent-based modeling, or system dynamics, Python can handle it all. You can draw on libraries like NumPy, SymPy, and SciPy to solve complex equations and perform dynamic simulations.

With economic models at your fingertips, you have the power to predict economic trends, evaluate policy changes, and explore the consequences of various decisions. Your Python toolkit equips you with the means to create, analyze, and refine economic models, allowing you to uncover valuable insights and guide critical economic decisions.

Solving Economic Models

Solving economic models involves finding solutions to the equations that you've meticulously crafted. These solutions can reveal critical information about economic behavior, policy impacts, and decision-making. In econometrics, two primary methods for solving economic models are simulation and optimization.

Simulation: Unveiling the Dynamics of Economic Systems

Simulations allow you to understand the behavior of economic systems over time. Whether you're interested in how a market evolves or how a policy change impacts an economy, simulation is a powerful tool. Python provides you with libraries like NumPy, SciPy, and SimPy to create dynamic simulations.

One common approach to simulation is Monte Carlo simulation. In this method, you repeatedly sample from probability distributions for key variables in your model. By aggregating these samples, you can observe the behavior of your economic system under different scenarios. For instance, you can use Monte Carlo simulation to assess the risk and return of various investment portfolios.

Here's a simplified Python example of a Monte Carlo simulation to estimate the expected return of an investment portfolio:

```python
import numpy as np

# Define parameters
mean_return = 0.12
std_dev = 0.18
initial_investment = 10000
investment_horizon = 5  # in years

# Number of simulations
num_simulations = 1000

# Simulate portfolio returns
simulated_returns = np.random.normal(mean_return, std_dev, (investment_horizon, num_simulations))
```

```python
# Calculate portfolio values over time
portfolio_values = initial_investment * np.cumprod(1 +
simulated_returns, axis=0)
```

```python
# Analyze results
expected_portfolio_value = np.mean(portfolio_values, axis=1)
```

Optimization: Finding the Best Solutions

Optimization is another critical tool in the economist's toolkit. It involves identifying the best possible outcomes or decision variables given constraints. In the realm of economics, this can translate to determining the optimal allocation of resources, setting prices to maximize profit, or finding the most efficient policy interventions.

Python offers numerous optimization libraries, including SciPy, PuLP, and CVXPY. These libraries can help you solve linear and nonlinear programming problems, constrained optimization, and more.

For instance, if you're working on a cost-minimization problem, you can employ optimization techniques to find the least expensive way to produce a certain level of output. Consider the following Python example:

python

```python
from scipy.optimize import minimize
```

```python
# Define cost function
```

```
def cost_function(x):
    return 2 * x + 3 * x  # Objective function to minimize

# Define constraints
constraints = ({'type': 'eq', 'fun': lambda x: 5 - x - x})

# Initial guess
initial_guess =

# Solve the optimization problem
result    =    minimize(cost_function,    initial_guess,
constraints=constraints)

# Extract the optimal solution
optimal_solution = result.x
```

In this example, we're minimizing a cost function while satisfying a constraint. The optimization process helps you find the combination of input values that minimizes the cost, making it a valuable technique for decision-making in economics.

By combining the power of simulation and optimization, you can explore various economic scenarios, evaluate policies, and optimize resource allocation. The ability to simulate economic systems and find optimal solutions empowers you to make data-driven decisions with confidence.

Conducting Simulations

As we venture further into the realm of economic

modeling, we now turn our focus to conducting economic simulations. Economic simulations are powerful tools that enable economists and data scientists to explore the behavior of complex systems, assess the impact of various policies, and make informed decisions. In this section, we will walk you through the steps for conducting economic simulations effectively.

Step 1: Define The Objectives

Every simulation begins with a clear understanding of the objectives. What do you aim to achieve with your simulation? Are you trying to model the effects of a specific economic policy, understand market dynamics, or forecast future trends? By defining your objectives, you set the stage for the entire simulation process.

Step 2: Model Specification

With your objectives in mind, the next crucial step is to specify the model. In other words, you need to define the components and relationships within the economic system you are simulating. This involves setting up equations, parameters, and variables that represent the dynamics of your economic model.

For example, if you are simulating the impact of changes in interest rates on consumer spending, you would need to define equations that describe the relationships between interest rates, disposable income, and consumer expenditures. This is where the modeling skills discussed in the earlier sections come into play.

Step 3: Data Collection And Calibration

Accurate and reliable data is the lifeblood of any economic simulation. You'll need historical data to calibrate your model and estimate model parameters. For instance, if you are modeling inflation, you might need historical inflation rates, central bank interest rates, and other relevant economic indicators. This data will be used to estimate the parameters in your model.

Python offers a wealth of data analysis tools and libraries, such as pandas, to help you collect and preprocess data efficiently. You can also visualize the data using libraries like Matplotlib and Seaborn to gain insights into its behavior.

Step 4: Choose A Simulation Approach

Economic simulations can take various forms, depending on the complexity of the model and the objectives. Two common approaches are:

Agent-Based Modeling (ABM): In ABM, you create individual agents (representing economic entities or individuals) and define their behavior. Agents interact with one another according to predefined rules. This approach is useful for modeling complex systems with numerous interacting components.

System Dynamics: System dynamics uses differential equations to represent the relationships between variables in an economic system. It is particularly suited for modeling dynamic systems with feedback loops, such as supply chains or market dynamics.

Your choice of simulation approach should align with your

objectives and the nature of the economic system you are modeling. Python provides libraries like Mesa for ABM and a range of tools for solving differential equations, making it a versatile choice for both approaches.

Step 5: Implement The Simulation

This step involves translating your model into Python code. You will need to create functions or classes to represent the components of your model, set up the simulation environment, and define the rules governing how the model evolves over time. Here's a simplified example of an ABM in Python:

python

```
import mesa
from mesa import Agent, Model
from mesa.time import RandomActivation
from mesa.space import MultiGrid

# Define the Agent class
class EconomicAgent(Agent):
    def __init__(self, unique_id, model):
        super().__init__(unique_id, model)
        self.wealth = 1

    def step(self):
        if self.wealth > 0:
            neighbor                                      =
self.random.choice(self.model.schedule.agents)
            neighbor.wealth += 1
```

```
        self.wealth -= 1

# Define the Model class
class EconomicModel(Model):
    def __init__(self, N, width, height):
        self.num_agents = N
        self.grid = MultiGrid(width, height, True)
        self.schedule = RandomActivation(self)

        # Create agents
        for i in range(self.num_agents):
            a = EconomicAgent(i, self)
            x = self.random.randrange(self.grid.width)
            y = self.random.randrange(self.grid.height)
            self.grid.place_agent(a, (x, y))
            self.schedule.add(a)

    def step(self):
        self.schedule.step()

# Create and run the model
model = EconomicModel(100, 10, 10)
for i in range(100):
    model.step()
```

In this basic example, agents interact by redistributing their wealth. Real-world simulations can be significantly more complex, but this simple case illustrates the structure of an ABM in Python.

Step 6: Run The Simulation

Once your simulation is implemented, it's time to run it. Simulations may require substantial computational resources, especially if they involve a large number of agents or complex computations. Python's multiprocessing capabilities can help speed up the simulation by distributing the workload across multiple CPU cores.

Step 7: Collect And Analyze Results

After running the simulation, collect the results and analyze the data. Python provides a wide array of libraries for data analysis and visualization, such as pandas, Num

Simulation Analysis and Interpretation (1,300 words)

In the world of econometrics and data science, simulation is a powerful tool to understand complex economic systems and make informed decisions. In the previous sections of this chapter, we've discussed building economic models, solving them, and conducting simulations. Now, it's time to delve into the crucial phase of simulation analysis and interpretation.

Simulation results can provide valuable insights into the behavior of economic systems, the effects of policies, and potential outcomes. However, these results are only as good as the analysis and interpretation that follows. In this section, we'll explore how to effectively make sense of your simulation data and draw meaningful conclusions.

Understanding the Simulation Output

Before diving into the analysis, it's essential to understand the nature of your simulation output. In most cases, simulation results are a collection of data points generated over numerous iterations. These data points could represent various economic indicators, such as GDP growth, inflation rates, unemployment rates, or stock prices, depending on the context of your simulation.

To illustrate the analysis process, let's consider a simplified example. Imagine you've developed a simulation model to study the impact of a new tax policy on consumer spending. Your model might produce data on consumer expenditures, tax revenue, and other relevant variables for multiple scenarios.

Descriptive Analysis

The first step in analyzing your simulation results is to perform descriptive analysis. This involves calculating basic statistics such as means, medians, standard deviations, and percentiles for your data. Descriptive statistics help you get a sense of the central tendencies, variations, and distribution of your simulation outcomes.

For our tax policy simulation, you might calculate the average change in consumer spending, the range of tax revenue variation, and the level of consumer expenditure volatility across different scenarios.

Visualization Techniques

Visualizing your simulation results can be immensely helpful in gaining a deeper understanding of the data. Python offers powerful libraries like Matplotlib and Seaborn to create a wide range of plots and graphs. Visualizations can reveal trends, patterns, and outliers that might not be immediately evident in tabular data.

Consider creating line charts to track how consumer spending and tax revenue change over time in response to the tax policy. Box plots can help you identify the spread and central values of these economic indicators under different conditions.

Hypothesis Testing

Depending on the complexity of your simulation, you might want to formulate and test hypotheses. Hypothesis testing allows you to make statistically supported claims about your simulation results. For instance, you could test whether the new tax policy has a significant impact on consumer spending or if the changes observed are within the realm of chance.

In Python, you can use libraries like SciPy to perform various hypothesis tests. The choice of the test will depend on the specific question you want to address and the type of data you've collected.

Sensitivity Analysis

Economic systems are often influenced by a multitude of factors, and small changes in parameters can lead to different outcomes. Sensitivity analysis helps you explore how sensitive your model is to parameter variations. This analysis involves systematically adjusting the parameters of your simulation and observing the corresponding changes in the results.

For the tax policy example, you could perform sensitivity analysis by altering the tax rates and observing how consumer spending and tax revenue respond. Sensitivity analysis provides insights into the robustness of your conclusions and helps identify critical parameters.

Scenario Comparison

Simulations often involve comparing multiple scenarios to evaluate the effectiveness of different policies or strategies. In Python, you can use Pandas and NumPy to organize your data and calculate various performance metrics for each scenario.

For the tax policy simulation, you might want to compare scenarios with different tax rates or tax structures to determine which one is most effective in achieving the desired economic outcomes.

Interpreting Implications

Once you've conducted your analysis, it's time to interpret the implications of your simulation results. What do the statistics, visualizations, and hypothesis tests tell you about the economic system you've modeled? Do the results support or challenge your initial hypotheses or policy objectives?

In the context of the tax policy simulation, your analysis might reveal that a specific tax rate leads to a noticeable increase in consumer spending but results in a smaller-than-expected increase in tax revenue. This finding could have implications for policymakers who seek to stimulate economic growth without compromising revenue streams.

Decision-Making and Policy Recommendations

Ultimately, the goal of simulation analysis is to inform decision-making. Based on your findings and interpretations, you can develop policy recommendations or strategies. These recommendations should be grounded in the evidence provided by your simulation, supported by rigorous analysis, and aligned with the objectives of your economic model.

For the tax policy simulation, you may recommend adopting the tax rate that maximizes consumer spending while carefully considering its impact on tax revenue. This recommendation can be crucial for policymakers and stakeholders seeking to strike a balance between economic growth and fiscal responsibility.

Simulation analysis and interpretation are integral parts of the economic modeling and data analysis process. Python's rich ecosystem of data science libraries empowers you to perform in-depth analysis, visualize results, test hypotheses, and make data-driven recommendations. By following these steps and utilizing Python's capabilities, you can unlock the full potential of simulations in the realm of econometrics and contribute to evidence-based decision-making.

Real-world Policy Simulation

In the world of econometrics and data-driven decision-making, the ability to simulate and analyze the effects of policy changes is invaluable. It allows economists and policymakers to foresee potential consequences and make informed choices that can shape the economic landscape. In this section, we will explore the process of conducting a real-world policy simulation using Python and econometric modeling.

Selecting the Policy of Interest

Before delving into the world of simulation, the first step is to identify and select the policy that you wish to analyze. The policy could be related to taxation, government spending, trade regulations, or any other economic variable. The choice of policy should align with the specific economic question you aim to answer.

For the purpose of our discussion, let's assume we are interested in exploring the effects of a tax cut on a country's GDP growth. The policy change, in this case, involves reducing tax rates across income brackets.

Defining the Economic Model

A sound economic model forms the basis for your simulation. It should represent the key relationships between economic variables affected by the chosen policy. Python offers various modeling libraries and tools that can be instrumental in creating econometric models.

In our example, you might design a model that includes variables like consumer spending, investment, and government revenue. You would define how these variables are interrelated and specify their reactions to changes in tax rates. Your model could take the form of equations or a system of equations that represent the economic dynamics.

Gathering Data and Parameters

Economic modeling and simulations rely heavily on data. You'll need to collect historical data to calibrate your model and estimate its parameters. Python's data manipulation libraries, such as Pandas, are invaluable for managing and analyzing datasets.

For our tax cut simulation, you would require historical data on GDP growth, tax rates, and other relevant economic indicators. This data is used to estimate the relationships in your model and to set the initial conditions for the simulation.

Simulation Setup

With the model and data in place, it's time to set up your simulation. Python provides libraries like NumPy that are ideal for handling numerical simulations. Your simulation should define a time frame and iterate over it to observe how the economy evolves in response to the policy change.

In the case of a tax cut, you would specify the starting year and iterate through subsequent years, adjusting tax rates each year to reflect the policy change. After each iteration, the model calculates the impact on GDP growth and updates the relevant variables.

Monte Carlo Simulations

Real-world policy simulations often face uncertainty due to various factors, such as changing consumer behavior or external economic shocks. Monte Carlo simulations are a valuable technique in econometrics. They involve running multiple simulations with random variations in input parameters to capture this uncertainty.

In Python, you can use libraries like NumPy to introduce randomness into your simulations. By performing multiple iterations with slightly different parameter values, you obtain a distribution of potential outcomes. This allows you to gauge the range of possible effects of the policy change.

Collecting and Analyzing Results

As your simulation runs, it generates a wealth of data. You'll need to collect and organize this data for analysis. Pandas is a powerful library for handling and analyzing simulation output, as it enables you to manipulate, filter, and summarize the data.

For our tax cut simulation, you might track and record GDP growth rates, government revenues, and other relevant metrics over time. By analyzing this data, you can observe the economic impact of the tax policy change.

Visualization for Clarity

Visualizing simulation results is crucial for understanding and communicating the findings. Python offers versatile libraries like Matplotlib and Seaborn for creating various types of plots. You can use line charts to visualize the trajectory of GDP growth, or bar charts to show the change in government revenue.

These visual representations help convey the effects of the policy change to a broader audience, including policymakers and stakeholders who may not be well-versed in econometrics.

Hypothesis Testing and Sensitivity Analysis

Once you've collected and visualized your simulation results, you can apply hypothesis testing to determine whether the observed effects of the policy change are statistically significant.

Python's libraries, such as SciPy, can aid in conducting hypothesis tests and calculating p-values.

Sensitivity analysis is also vital to understand how sensitive your model is to variations in parameter values. By altering assumptions and parameters within a reasonable range, you can assess the robustness of your findings.

Interpreting the Policy Implications

Now comes the critical step of interpreting your results. What do the simulation outcomes tell you about the impact of the tax cut policy? How significant are the changes in GDP growth and government revenue? Are there unexpected consequences, such as an increase in consumer spending or a decline in savings?

The interpretation phase may involve discussing the economic implications of your findings and their relevance to real-world decision-making. It's important to provide context for your results and consider the broader economic landscape.

Policy Recommendations

Based on your analysis and interpretation, you can formulate policy recommendations. These recommendations should be rooted in the evidence generated by your simulation. They should consider the intended and unintended consequences of the policy change and provide guidance to policymakers.

In the case of our tax cut simulation, you might recommend proceeding with the tax cut if it leads to a significant boost in GDP growth. However, you should also highlight potential risks, such as reduced government revenue, and suggest strategies to mitigate these risks.

Ethical Considerations

In the modern world of econometrics, ethical considerations are paramount. It's important to examine the ethical implications of the policy change and ensure that it aligns with principles of fairness and social responsibility.

Consider whether the tax cut disproportionately benefits certain income groups or has unintended negative consequences for vulnerable populations. Python can assist in quantifying and analyzing these ethical aspects within your simulation framework.

Real-world policy simulations are a cornerstone of modern economic analysis and decision-making. Python, with its extensive ecosystem of libraries, empowers economists to build models, run simulations, and derive meaningful insights. By following the steps outlined in this section, you can explore the potential impacts of policy changes and contribute to informed, data-driven policy decisions that shape the economic landscape.

Conclusion and Policy Recommendations

As we draw the curtain on our journey through Python in Econometrics, it's time to synthesize our findings and derive actionable policy recommendations from the simulations we've conducted. We've explored the realms of economic modeling and simulation, understanding their power in shaping policy decisions. In this concluding section, we'll summarize the key takeaways and offer guidance for policymakers based on the results of our simulations.

Summarizing the Findings

Throughout this book, we've embarked on a comprehensive exploration of Python's role in the world of econometrics. We've delved into the fundamentals of Python, data preparation, basic econometric analysis, time series analysis, panel data, advanced econometric techniques, and even machine learning. We've built economic models, conducted simulations, and visualized data to reveal insights that bridge data science and economic analysis.

In this final section, let's revisit some of the core findings:

Python, with its rich libraries and versatility, has emerged as a powerful tool for economists. Its capacity to seamlessly integrate with data science techniques has revolutionized econometric analysis.

Data preparation is the foundation for sound econometric analysis. Techniques such as data cleaning, transformation, and visualization are vital steps in extracting meaningful insights from data.

Basic econometric analysis, including linear and multiple regression, has provided us with essential tools for modeling and prediction. Model validation and real-world applications have cemented our understanding of these techniques.

Time series analysis has equipped us with the ability to tackle temporal data, decompose it into its components, and forecast future trends, with practical applications in stock price forecasting.

Panel data analysis, with fixed and random effects models, has broadened our horizons, allowing us to explore multi-dimensional datasets and understand individual heterogeneity.

Advanced econometric techniques, like instrumental variable regression and limited dependent variable models, have given us powerful tools for addressing complex real-world problems.

Machine learning, a significant player in modern econometrics, has shown us how to employ supervised and unsupervised learning for economic prediction.

We've also delved into policy impact assessment, understanding how to evaluate the effects of interventions using instrumental variable regression.

The book concludes with economic modeling and simulations, revealing the potential consequences of policy changes through data-driven analysis.

These key takeaways serve as a foundation for our policy recommendations. But remember, with great power comes great responsibility. As we transition to policy recommendations, let's keep in mind the ethical considerations that govern the choices we make.

Policy Recommendations

Now, let's step into the shoes of a policymaker, armed with the insights derived from our simulations. It's essential to remember that the impact of policy changes is multifaceted, and our recommendations should reflect this complexity.

Data-Driven Policy Design: Our simulations have emphasized

the importance of basing policy decisions on solid data. We recommend that policymakers prioritize data collection, analysis, and interpretation. Use Python and its data science capabilities to assess the potential effects of proposed policies rigorously.

Caution in Tax Policy Changes: For instance, consider our simulated tax cut scenario. The results showed that a tax cut can stimulate GDP growth, but it also led to reduced government revenue. Our recommendation is to proceed with caution when implementing tax cuts, ensuring that the lost revenue doesn't compromise essential public services.

Monitoring and Adaptation: The real-world is dynamic. Our simulations are based on historical data and assumptions. We recommend continuous monitoring of policy effects and readiness to adapt as needed. Python can be your ally in creating real-time dashboards and automated data analysis.

Balancing Economic Growth and Equity: In the pursuit of economic growth, policymakers must not forget equity. As you have seen, policy changes can have differential impacts on various population segments. We recommend a commitment to fairness and measures to mitigate potential inequalities.

Machine Learning for Predictive Governance: Our exploration of machine learning showcased its potential in economic prediction. We recommend the integration of machine learning models in forecasting economic trends, such as inflation rates or labor market behavior.

Ethical Considerations: Machine learning applications must be accompanied by rigorous ethical guidelines. Bias and fairness issues should be addressed, and algorithms should be transparent and accountable.

Evidence-Based Decision-Making: Our analysis has underscored the value of evidence-based decision-making. We recommend that policymakers develop a culture of utilizing data-driven insights when crafting policies. This will enhance their efficacy and public trust.

Comprehensive Economic Models: Our examination of economic modeling and simulations revealed their power in anticipating policy impacts. Policymakers are encouraged to create comprehensive economic models for a more profound understanding of potential consequences.

Simulation-based Policy Testing: Prior to implementing significant policy changes, consider running simulations to gauge potential outcomes. These simulations can serve as a valuable decision support tool.

Communication and Transparency: When policy changes are introduced, effective communication with the public is essential. We recommend transparency in outlining the objectives, methods, and expected outcomes of policy changes.

In Closing

Python in Econometrics has equipped you with a formidable set of tools. You've journeyed through data science techniques, advanced econometrics, and machine learning, all while maintaining a commitment to ethical considerations. Your understanding of economic modeling and simulations is a testament to the potential for informed decision-making.

As we conclude this book, keep in mind that Python's role in the world of econometrics is ever-evolving. Staying updated with the latest libraries, techniques, and best practices is essential. This knowledge will enable you to adapt to the dynamic economic landscape and continue making a meaningful impact as an economist.

Whether you're a student, an economist, or a policymaker, the insights you've gained here will serve as a valuable asset in the realms of economics, data science, and policy. We look forward to seeing how you apply these learnings to shape a brighter economic future.

CHAPTER 9: DATA VISUALIZATION AND REPORTING

In the vast landscape of data, the ability to effectively communicate insights is paramount. As we step into Chapter 9, we explore the art and science of data visualization and reporting. Here, we delve into advanced techniques for transforming data into compelling visual narratives, interactive dashboards, and persuasive reports. Join us on a journey through the world of data presentation, where the visual medium takes center stage to convey complex economic stories with clarity and impact.

Advanced Data Visualization

Data visualization is the art of transforming raw data into meaningful insights. In this chapter, we venture into the realm of advanced data visualization, where we harness the power of Python libraries such as Seaborn and Plotly to create visual representations that not only elucidate complex economic data but do so in an engaging and captivating manner.

Seaborn: A Symphony of Visual Elegance

Seaborn, a Python data visualization library, is a masterful conductor that can turn your data into a symphony of graphs and charts. With its high-level interface, Seaborn simplifies the process of creating stunning visualizations. It provides a plethora of color palettes and styles, allowing you to tailor your visualizations to your audience and the story you want to tell.

Let's explore some of the remarkable capabilities of Seaborn:

1. Distplot - The Maestro of Distributions

Imagine having the ability to not only visualize your data but also comprehend its underlying distribution. Seaborn's distplot function grants you this power. By combining a histogram with a kernel density estimate, it elegantly showcases the probability density of your data.

Here's a quick example to whet your appetite:

python

```
import seaborn as sns
import matplotlib.pyplot as plt

# Create a sample dataset
data =

# Create a distribution plot
sns.set(style="whitegrid")
sns.distplot(data, kde=True, color="skyblue")

# Add labels for clarity
```

```python
plt.xlabel("Value")
plt.ylabel("Density")
plt.title("Distribution of Sample Data")
plt.show()
```

This concise code generates a beautiful distribution plot, offering both insights and aesthetic appeal.

2. Pairplot - The Ensemble of Relationships

Another treasure within Seaborn's chest is the pairplot. It's your ensemble conductor, orchestrating a visual exploration of relationships between variables. With just a few lines of code, you can create a matrix of scatterplots and histograms for multiple variables, shedding light on correlations and patterns in your data.

Consider this example:

python

```python
import seaborn as sns
import matplotlib.pyplot as plt

# Load a sample dataset
data = sns.load_dataset("iris")

# Create a pairplot
sns.set(style="ticks")
sns.pairplot(data, hue="species")
```

```python
# Add some final touches
plt.suptitle("Pairplot of Iris Dataset", y=1.02)
plt.show()
```

The pairplot takes your dataset on a visual journey, highlighting relationships, clusters, and differences.

Plotly: Interactivity in Concert

If Seaborn is the master of elegance, Plotly is the virtuoso of interactivity. As we progress through the chapter, you will learn how Plotly's interactive visualizations can take your data storytelling to the next level. Be prepared to create dynamic plots that your audience can explore and interact with, fostering deeper engagement and understanding.

We'll walk through a quick example of a Plotly scatter plot. First, you'll need to install Plotly:

bash

```bash
pip install plotly
```

Now, let's create a simple scatter plot:

python

```python
import plotly.express as px

# Sample data
import pandas as pd
```

```
data = pd.DataFrame({
    'X': ,
    'Y':
})
```

```
# Create a scatter plot
fig = px.scatter(data, x='X', y='Y', title='Scatter Plot with Plotly')
fig.show()
```

The Plotly scatter plot comes to life in your web browser, and you can hover over points for details, zoom in and out, or pan for closer inspection. This interactivity brings your data to life and provides a captivating experience for your audience.

A Symphony of Visualization

In this section, we've merely scratched the surface of what Seaborn and Plotly can achieve in the realm of data visualization. As you delve deeper into this chapter, you'll harness the full potential of these libraries to craft visual stories that resonate with your readers. We'll explore various chart types, customization options, and interactivity features to ensure your data speaks with eloquence.

Prepare to be a virtuoso of data visualization, wielding the instruments of Seaborn and Plotly to convey intricate economic insights with clarity and beauty. The stage is set, the curtains drawn, and the orchestra ready to perform. Let the visualization symphony begin!

Interactive Visualizations: Unveiling the Power of Interactivity

As we've progressed through the world of data science and econometrics, you've learned how to create captivating visualizations using Python libraries like Seaborn and Plotly. These visualizations have allowed you to convey complex economic data with clarity and precision. Now, it's time to take your skills to the next level by exploring the realm of interactive visualizations and data dashboards.

Interactive visualizations are like magic spells for engaging your audience. They allow s to interact with the data, explore various scenarios, and gain deeper insights. In this section, we'll delve into the art of crafting interactive data visualizations and dynamic dashboards using Python.

Plotly: Your Wand for Interactivity

To bring interactivity to your visualizations, we turn to Plotly, the enchanting library that empowers you to create dynamic charts and dashboards. With Plotly, your static visualizations come alive, enabling your audience to explore data with just a click or a hover.

Let's embark on an example of creating an interactive scatter plot using Plotly:

python

```
import plotly.express as px

# Sample data
import pandas as pd
data = pd.DataFrame({
```

'X': ,

'Y': ,

'Label':

})

Create an interactive scatter plot

fig = px.scatter(data, x='X', y='Y', text='Label', title='Interactive Scatter Plot with Plotly')

Add interactivity: hover, zoom, pan

fig.update_traces(textposition='top center', textfont_size=12, marker=dict(size=12, opacity=0.7))

Display the magic!

fig.show()

This code conjures an interactive scatter plot. When your readers hover over data points, they reveal labels, and they can zoom and pan for a closer look.

Dash: Crafting Dynamic Data Dashboards

Now, let's venture into the world of Dash, a Python framework for building interactive web applications. With Dash, you can create data dashboards that offer a wide range of interactive components like sliders, dropdowns, and buttons. These dashboards provide a -friendly interface for exploring data and gaining insights.

Here's a glimpse of what Dash can do:

python

```python
import dash
import dash_core_components as dcc
import dash_html_components as html
from dash.dependencies import Input, Output

app = dash.Dash(__name__)

# Define the layout of the dashboard
app.layout = html.Div()

# Define callback to update the graph based on input
@app.callback(
    Output('economic-visual', 'figure'),

)
def update_graph(selected_year):
    # Code to update the graph based on the selected year
    # Example: You could filter and plot data for the selected year
    return updated_figure

# Run the app
if __name__ == '__main__':
    app.run_server(debug=True)
```

This code creates a simple economic data dashboard with a slider to choose the year. As you slide through different years, the data visualizations will dynamically update, allowing you to explore economic trends over time.

Weaving Stories with Interactivity

Interactive visualizations and dashboards aren't just fancy bells and whistles; they serve a crucial purpose in data analysis and communication. They let you tell stories with your data, enabling your readers to become active participants in the narrative.

Imagine presenting a report on the impact of economic policies with a dynamic dashboard. Decision-makers can explore scenarios, adjust parameters, and see the immediate effects. This level of engagement can lead to more informed decisions and deeper insights.

As you master the art of crafting interactive data visualizations and dashboards, remember that the key is to design for your audience. Think about what questions they might have and how interactivity can help answer them. Ensure that your visuals are clear, intuitive, and responsive to actions.

This section has equipped you with the tools and knowledge to make your data come to life. Now, go forth and weave interactive stories with your data, engaging your audience in a way that traditional static charts never could. The magic of interactivity is at your fingertips, and it's time to cast your spell on the world of econometrics.

Reporting Results: Crafting Persuasive Data Narratives in Jupyter Notebooks

In the realm of data science and econometrics, the ability to effectively communicate your findings is just as important as the analysis itself. You've harnessed the power of Python to wrangle, visualize, and model economic data, but your journey is far from complete. Now, it's time to explore the art of presenting and reporting results, and what better platform for this task than Jupyter Notebooks.

Jupyter Notebooks are the canvas upon which you paint the story of your data analysis. They allow you to blend code, visualizations, and textual explanations into a seamless narrative that guides your readers through your analytical journey. In this section, we'll unravel the secrets of creating compelling data reports in Jupyter Notebooks.

The Structure of a Jupyter Notebook

Before we dive into the details, let's take a moment to understand the basic structure of a Jupyter Notebook. A Jupyter Notebook is organized into cells, which can be of two primary types: code cells and markdown cells.

Code Cells: These are where you write and execute your Python code. They are the computational engine of your notebook, allowing you to perform data analysis, run models, and generate visualizations.

Markdown Cells: These are where the magic of storytelling happens. Markdown cells contain text, explanations, and formatted content. You can use markdown to provide context, describe your analysis, interpret results, and create an engaging narrative.

The flow of a Jupyter Notebook typically follows a logical sequence:

Introduction: Begin with a markdown cell that introduces your analysis. What's the problem you're tackling? What's the goal of your analysis? Provide a roadmap for your readers.

Data Preparation: If you have data cleaning or preprocessing steps, document them in code cells. Ensure you use clear comments to explain each step.

Data Exploration: Visualize and explore your data using code cells for generating plots. Use markdown cells to provide interpretations. You can use libraries like Matplotlib and Seaborn for visualizations.

Modeling and Analysis: Perform your econometric analysis. Write code to run regressions, time series models, or any other analysis you've been working on. Explain your model choices, assumptions, and methodology in markdown cells.

Results: Present the results of your analysis in a clear and concise manner. This can be a mix of code cells (for displaying numerical results) and markdown cells (for explaining what the results mean).

Discussion: Offer insights, interpretations, and the real-world implications of your findings. Use markdown to tell a data-driven story.

Conclusion: Summarize your analysis and its key takeaways. Markdown cells are perfect for this. What did you discover, and what should your readers remember?

References: If you referred to external sources, include them in a markdown cell. It's good practice to cite your references.

Presenting Data with Markdown

Markdown is your literary tool to weave the narrative within your Jupyter Notebook. Here are some tips to create engaging and informative content:

Clarity and Simplicity: Use clear and simple language. Avoid jargon unless it's necessary and defined. Remember, your goal is to make your analysis accessible to a broad audience.

Visual Enhancements: Make your text visually appealing. Use headers to structure your content, bullet points or numbered lists for clarity, and emphasize important points with bold or italics. Consider adding images, diagrams, or tables to enhance understanding.

Interactive Widgets: Jupyter Notebooks allow you to include interactive widgets like sliders, dropdowns, or buttons. These can be used to give your readers a hands-on experience in exploring data or adjusting parameters.

Equations and Formulas: If your analysis involves mathematical equations, Markdown supports LaTeX for rendering beautiful mathematical expressions.

markdown

For example, you can write the formula for the mean as:
$$\bar{x} = \frac{1}{n}\sum_{i=1}^{n} x_i$$

Hyperlinks: Include hyperlinks to external resources, references, or related articles. You can create clickable links like this: Example Link.

Code Cells: A Glimpse into the Analysis

While Markdown cells form the backbone of your data report, don't forget the significance of code cells. They provide transparency and reproducibility to your analysis. When using code cells in your analysis, consider the following:

Code Organization: Keep your code organized. Use comments to explain complex logic and include variable names that are descriptive and meaningful.

Consistency: Stick to a consistent style when writing your code. Follow Python's PEP 8 style guide for code formatting.

Error Handling: Anticipate potential errors and use exception handling to make your code robust. Explain how you handle errors in your markdown cells.

Intermediate Outputs: If your code generates intermediate outputs or plots, it's often helpful to include these in your report. Visualizations and intermediate results can serve as a bridge between code and narrative.

Sharing Your Jupyter Notebook

Once you've created your data report in Jupyter Notebook, it's time to share it with the world. Jupyter Notebooks can be easily shared through platforms like Jupyter Notebook Viewer, GitHub, or by converting them to HTML or PDF for wider distribution.

Remember to provide clear instructions for running the notebook, especially if it involves external data sources or specific dependencies.

In this section, we've explored the art of presenting and reporting results in Jupyter Notebooks. Whether you're sharing your findings with colleagues, decision-makers, or the broader public, Jupyter Notebooks offer a versatile platform to tell the story of your data analysis. By skillfully combining code and narrative, you can create persuasive data reports that enlighten and engage, transforming your data into a compelling tale. So, go forth and let your data speak through the eloquence of Jupyter Notebooks. Your insights await their audience.

Report Exporting and Sharing

.

Before you can share your reports, you need to decide on the best format for your content. Python offers several options for exporting your visualizations and reports. Let's explore some of the most common ones:

HTML Reports: You can export your Jupyter Notebook as an HTML file, which can be easily shared with others. This format retains the interactive elements of your notebook, making it a powerful choice for reports with interactive charts and widgets.

PDF Documents: For a more traditional and printable format, exporting your report as a PDF is a great option. You can use libraries like Matplotlib, Seaborn, and Pandas to generate static plots that can be included in a PDF.

Interactive Dashboards: If you want to create interactive dashboards, tools like Plotly, Dash, or Bokeh are excellent choices. These libraries allow you to build web-based interactive applications that can be easily shared via a web link.

Image Files: Sometimes, you may need to use images in presentations or documents. You can export Matplotlib or Seaborn plots as image files, such as PNG or JPEG.

LaTeX Documents: If your report involves complex mathematical formulas and you prefer a document format, you can export your content to a LaTeX document, ensuring high-quality typesetting.

Exporting Reports as HTML

Creating HTML reports from Jupyter Notebooks is a practical way to share your interactive visualizations and analysis. Here's how you can do it:

python

```
# Exporting a Jupyter Notebook as an HTML report
!jupyter nbconvert --to html Your_Notebook.ipynb
```

This command will generate an HTML file that retains your code, visualizations, and explanations. You can then share this HTML file with others, and they can view it using a web browser.

Exporting Reports as PDF

To create a PDF report from your Jupyter Notebook, you can use the nbconvert tool with LaTeX. First, you'll need to install the required packages:

python

!pip install nbconvert

!apt-get install texlive-xetex texlive-fonts-recommended texlive-generic-recommended

After installation, run the following command:

python

```
# Exporting a Jupyter Notebook as a PDF report
!jupyter nbconvert --to pdf Your_Notebook.ipynb
```

This will generate a PDF file with your content, which you can share with colleagues or stakeholders.

Building Interactive Dashboards

If you want to create interactive dashboards to share your data and visualizations, tools like Plotly, Dash, and Bokeh are excellent choices. These libraries allow you to build web-based applications that can be accessed via a web link. s can interact with your visualizations, changing parameters, and exploring data on their own.

For example, with Plotly and Dash, you can create an interactive web application like this:

python

```
# Creating a simple Dash dashboard
```

```
import dash
import dash_core_components as dcc
import dash_html_components as html

app = dash.Dash(__name__)

app.layout = html.Div()

if __name__ == '__main__':
    app.run_server(debug=True)
```

By running this code, you'll create an interactive web dashboard. s can access it through a URL, allowing you to share your analysis with a broader audience.

Sharing Your Work

Once you've exported your reports or created interactive dashboards, it's time to share them with your intended audience. Here are some tips on sharing your work effectively:

Version Control: Use version control systems like Git and platforms like GitHub to track changes and collaborate with others.

Cloud Platforms: Upload your reports to cloud storage services like Google Drive, Dropbox, or GitHub. This ensures accessibility and easy sharing.

Shareable Links: If you've built web-based dashboards, share the links with your audience, making it easy for them to access and explore the data.

Documentation: Include clear documentation to guide s on how to interact with your reports or dashboards. Explain the purpose and how to interpret the findings.

Feedback Loop: Encourage feedback from your audience. Constructive feedback can help improve your analysis and visualization for future reports.

The ability to export and share your reports and visualizations is crucial in the field of econometrics. Choose the right format for your audience, and leverage Python's libraries and tools to create interactive and informative reports. By following best practices in sharing and documentation, you ensure that your hard work has the impact it deserves. Whether it's an HTML report, a PDF document, or an interactive dashboard, your insights will reach the right eyes, enhancing your communication and decision-making in the field of economics.

Policy Brief and Communication

In the ever-evolving landscape of data science and econometrics, effective communication of your findings is an indispensable skill. It's not enough to crunch numbers and derive insightful conclusions; you must also be able to convey those insights in a way that is clear, compelling, and influential. This chapter delves into creating a policy brief using data visualization techniques, an essential tool for economists to communicate their results to a broader audience, including policymakers, stakeholders, and the general public.

Why Policy Briefs Matter

Imagine you've spent weeks, or even months, conducting a

rigorous econometric analysis to uncover significant trends or patterns in a complex economic issue. Your findings have the potential to drive impactful changes in economic policies. However, your work is futile if you cannot effectively communicate your insights to decision-makers, who may not have the same level of technical expertise.

Policy briefs serve as the bridge between your technical analysis and actionable change. These concise documents are designed to inform, persuade, and guide those in a position to implement real-world policies. As an economist, mastering the art of creating persuasive policy briefs is crucial, and data visualization plays a pivotal role in this process.

The Power of Data Visualization

Numbers and statistics alone can be overwhelming for policymakers or a lay audience. Data visualization offers a way to distill complex information into easily digestible visuals. Whether through charts, graphs, or interactive dashboards, you can present your findings in a manner that is not only informative but also engaging.

When preparing a policy brief, consider the following data visualization techniques:

Infographics: These are a powerful tool for simplifying complex information. You can use infographics to represent key statistics, trends, and comparisons in a visually appealing way. For instance, you might create an infographic showing the impact of a proposed policy change on different sectors of the economy.

Charts and Graphs: Visual representations such as bar charts, line graphs, and pie charts are great for illustrating trends and relationships within your data. When explaining how an economic variable has changed over time, a well-designed line graph can be much more impactful than a table of numbers.

Interactive Dashboards: If you're dealing with a wealth of data, interactive dashboards can allow policymakers to explore the data themselves. Tools like Tableau or Power BI enable you to create dynamic, -friendly interfaces for your data.

Geospatial Visualizations: If your analysis involves geographical data, consider using maps to display regional variations. Highlighting how economic conditions differ across regions can be particularly compelling.

Creating Your Policy Brief

Your policy brief should be succinct, focusing on the most critical points of your analysis. Typically, it should include the following components:

Title and Executive Summary: Begin with a clear and attention-grabbing title. Follow it with an executive summary that provides a concise overview of your analysis and key findings.

Introduction: Briefly introduce the problem or issue that your analysis addresses.

Methodology: Explain your approach and the data sources used for your analysis. This is where you establish your credibility.

Key Findings: Present your main findings using data visualization. Highlight the most significant trends and outcomes. Make sure these visuals are easy to interpret and aesthetically pleasing.

Policy Recommendations: Based on your analysis, offer clear and actionable policy recommendations. Your recommendations should be directly tied to the insights you've gained from your data.

Conclusion: Summarize your findings and recommendations. Emphasize the importance of your analysis and the potential impact of the proposed policies.

References: Include any sources you referenced in your analysis.

Remember that simplicity is key. Avoid cluttering your policy brief with excessive detail or overly complex visuals. Your goal is to guide your audience through your findings and persuade them to take action.

Let's look at a hypothetical example to illustrate the power of data visualization in a policy brief:

Hypothetical Scenario: You've conducted an econometric analysis of the impact of a new environmental regulation on different industries. Your analysis indicates that while some industries will face short-term challenges, the long-term benefits, such as reduced pollution and health care savings, far outweigh the initial costs.

In your policy brief, you might include a visually appealing bar chart showing the expected reduction in pollution levels over time and a pie chart demonstrating the potential savings in health care expenses. These visuals make your case more compelling than pages of raw data.

To further enhance your policy brief, consider utilizing Python for data visualization. The Matplotlib and Seaborn libraries offer versatile options for creating a wide range of charts and graphs. Below, we provide an example of how to create a simple line graph using Matplotlib:

```python
python

import matplotlib.pyplot as plt

years =
pollution_levels =

plt.plot(years, pollution_levels, marker='o', linestyle='-', color='b')
plt.title('Reduction in Pollution Over Time')
plt.xlabel('Year')
plt.ylabel('Pollution Levels')
plt.grid(True)
plt.show()
```

This code creates a visually appealing line graph showing the gradual reduction in pollution levels over a series of years. Such a visualization can effectively convey the positive effects of the proposed environmental regulation.

Mastering the art of data visualization is essential for

economists seeking to influence policy decisions. By distilling complex data into easily understandable visuals, you can ensure that your insights have a real impact on the economic landscape. Through this, you not only bridge the gap between your technical analysis and policymaking but also empower decision-makers to make informed choices for the betterment of society.

Real-world Visualization Case Study

In the realm of econometrics, the true power of data lies in its ability to transform complex numerical information into actionable insights that drive real change. To illustrate this transformative potential, we embark on a journey through a real-world case study where data visualization becomes the linchpin of policy communication.

The Case Study: Unveiling Income Inequality

Our case study revolves around the pressing issue of income inequality. This socioeconomic challenge has profound implications for policymakers, as addressing it effectively can lead to fairer, more equitable societies. Our mission is to uncover, analyze, and communicate insights regarding income inequality, shedding light on disparities and advocating for data-driven policies.

Understanding the Data

To address income inequality, we first need to gather relevant data. In our case, we've obtained comprehensive data sets containing income information across various demographics, regions, and socioeconomic groups. These data sources may include government surveys, census reports, or financial records.

Data Preparation and Exploration

Before diving into data visualization, we must prepare and explore the data. This process involves data cleaning, transformation, and initial analysis to understand the key trends and patterns. For instance, we might discover disparities in income distribution between urban and rural areas, among different age groups, or across various ethnic backgrounds.

Selecting the Right Visualizations

Data visualization is not just about making graphs; it's about selecting the right visualizations that best convey the information. In our case study, we employ a variety of visual elements to ensure comprehensive coverage:

Choropleth Maps: To highlight regional disparities in income, we use choropleth maps. These maps shade regions in different colors based on income levels, providing a clear visual representation of income distribution across the country.

Stacked Bar Charts: Stacked bar charts help us compare income sources and understand the composition of individuals' incomes. By breaking down income into categories like wages, investments, and government transfers, we can uncover the nuances in income sources.

Gini Coefficient Trends: The Gini coefficient is a common measure of income inequality. We create a line chart showing how the Gini coefficient has changed over the years. This visual representation illustrates whether income inequality is increasing, decreasing, or staying the same.

Demographic Pie Charts: To understand how income inequality affects different demographic groups, we use pie charts to show the distribution of income among various segments of the population. This helps us pinpoint where disparities are most significant.

Presenting the Findings

Effective data visualization is not only about creating compelling visuals but also about presenting them coherently. In our case study, we structure our presentation to ensure policymakers and the public can grasp the issue at a glance.

Introduction: We start with an introduction to the problem, explaining why income inequality is a critical issue.

Choropleth Maps: Our first set of visualizations involves choropleth maps, which vividly display regional disparities. Viewers can immediately discern the income inequality across states or regions.

Income Sources: The stacked bar charts reveal the sources of income for different demographic groups, emphasizing the diversity of income streams.

Gini Coefficient Trends: We use line charts to present Gini coefficient trends, which offer an overall perspective on income inequality's evolution.

Demographic Pie Charts: These charts highlight how income inequality affects specific demographic groups. The audience can see, for example, how income disparities vary among different age brackets or ethnic communities.

Policy Recommendations

A critical aspect of our case study is translating these insights into actionable policy recommendations. Our data visualization reveals not just the problems but also potential solutions.

Progressive Taxation: We propose a more progressive taxation system that imposes higher taxes on the wealthy, using the data to underscore the income gaps.

Targeted Welfare Programs: Data visualization showcases which demographic groups are most affected by income inequality, guiding policymakers in the design of more targeted welfare programs.

Minimum Wage Adjustments: Insights into income sources reveal that some individuals rely heavily on wages. We recommend periodic adjustments to the minimum wage to ensure that full-time work can support a decent standard of living.

Education and Skills Training: Demographic data help us pinpoint which groups are most affected by income disparities. We propose investing in education and skills training for these groups to enhance their earning potential.

The Impact of Visualization

Through data visualization, our case study effectively communicates the magnitude and nuances of income inequality. Policymakers and the public gain a deeper understanding of the issue, its causes, and potential solutions. They see the regional disparities, the varied income sources, and the trends over time, all of which inform and guide decisions.

Data visualization isn't just about making pretty charts; it's about translating data into actionable insights. In our case study, these insights form the basis for informed policy decisions that address the critical issue of income inequality. The power of data, when harnessed through effective visualization, becomes a potent instrument for change, shaping fairer and more equitable societies.

The real-world visualization case study on income inequality serves as a testament to the transformative power of data visualization in the field of econometrics. Through compelling choropleth maps, informative stacked bar charts, insightful Gini coefficient trends, and illuminating demographic pie charts, we have unveiled the complexities of income inequality. These visuals have not only highlighted the disparities but also presented a pathway to action.

By effectively communicating the magnitude and nuances of income inequality, we have provided policymakers and the public with a deeper understanding of this critical issue. It's not just about pretty charts; it's about translating data into actionable insights. These insights, in turn, become the cornerstone for informed policy decisions that have the potential to create fairer and more equitable societies.

The impact of data visualization extends far beyond aesthetics; it's about making data matter. As we move forward in our journey through "Python in Econometrics: Bridging Data Science and Economic Analysis," we carry with us the knowledge that data, when harnessed through effective visualization, becomes a potent instrument for change. It has the power to shape policies that address socioeconomic disparities and promote a more just and equitable world.

CHAPTER 10: BEST PRACTICES AND CONCLUSION

Welcome to the final chapter of "Python in Econometrics: Bridging Data Science and Economic Analysis." In Chapter 10, titled "Best Practices and Conclusion," we embark on a reflective journey through the essential principles, strategies, and insights that underpin the world of econometric analysis using Python. This concluding chapter serves as a compass, guiding you towards mastering the art of applying Python in econometrics, all while encouraging continuous growth and learning in this dynamic field.

As we bring this comprehensive guide to its closure, we will navigate through a spectrum of best practices for coding, analysis, and documentation. We'll delve into strategies for debugging and troubleshooting, ensuring that you have the tools and knowledge to navigate the intricate world of Python effectively. Moreover, we will explore the importance of staying updated with the latest Python libraries and techniques, given the ever-evolving landscape of data science and econometrics.

To conclude this enlightening journey, we'll summarize the key takeaways from the book, emphasizing the broader applications of Python in econometrics. You'll gain a holistic perspective of how Python can be leveraged not only in academic research but also in real-world scenarios, enabling you to harness its capabilities for impactful decision-making.

In the final section of this chapter, we'll provide you with a rich trove of additional resources, from books and courses to websites, for those eager to continue their learning journey. These resources will act as your stepping stones for further exploration, ensuring that your quest for mastery in Python-based econometric analysis continues long after you've completed this book.

So, fasten your seatbelt, as we set sail on a voyage through the best practices and key takeaways, culminating in a treasure trove of resources to equip you for your continued pursuit of excellence in Python and econometrics. Let's dive into Chapter 10 and embrace the culmination of your journey toward becoming a proficient economist and data scientist.

Best Practices

Adhering to best practices is not just a matter of preference; it's a fundamental requirement for producing reliable, accurate, and reproducible results. Whether you are an aspiring economist, a seasoned data scientist, or anyone in between, these best practices are your guiding principles, ensuring that your work stands on a solid foundation. In this section, we'll delve into a comprehensive summary of best practices for coding, analysis, and documentation in econometric analysis.

1. Code Clarity and Organization

Practice clean coding habits. Writing clear, well-organized code is the cornerstone of reproducible research. Utilize meaningful variable names, add comments for clarity, and break down complex tasks into modular functions.

Embrace consistency. Consistency in coding style and formatting is essential. Choose a code style guide, whether it's PEP 8 for Python or any other, and stick to it. Consistency simplifies code maintenance and collaboration.

2. Data Preprocessing and Cleaning

Start with quality data. The saying "garbage in, garbage out" holds true in econometrics. Ensure your data is accurate, complete, and free from errors. Implement rigorous data validation and preprocessing routines.

Handle missing data wisely. Decide whether to remove or impute missing data based on the context. Be transparent about your approach in your documentation.

3. Model Selection and Specification

Avoid overfitting. Overly complex models can lead to overfitting, where a model fits noise instead of the underlying patterns. Utilize techniques like cross-validation to determine the optimal model complexity.

Consider model assumptions. Most econometric models come with underlying assumptions that need to be validated. Assumptions can include linearity, independence of errors, and more. Ensure you assess and address any violations of these assumptions.

4. Documentation and Reproducibility

Document your code and analysis. Keep a clear record of your code and analysis steps. This not only aids your future self but also enables others to understand and reproduce your work.

Version control. Implement a version control system like Git to track changes in your code and analysis. This safeguards against unintended changes and facilitates collaboration.

5. Robustness Checks

Perform sensitivity analysis. Test the robustness of your results by changing assumptions or parameters. This practice helps determine how sensitive your findings are to variations in your model.

6. Communication

Craft clear and concise reports. Whether you're preparing a research paper, policy brief, or presentation, clarity in communication is key. Tailor your reports to your audience, explaining complex concepts in accessible language.

Visualize results. Use data visualization to convey your findings effectively. Graphics and charts can illuminate insights that might be obscured in dense tables.

7. Ethical Considerations

Address ethical considerations. In an age of increasing data and technology, it's crucial to consider ethical implications. Avoid bias, respect privacy, and promote fairness in your analysis.

Share your data. In line with ethical research practices, consider sharing your dataset (with personal information appropriately anonymized) to foster transparency and collaboration.

8. Continuous Learning

Stay updated. The world of data science and econometrics evolves rapidly. Invest time in staying updated with the latest tools, libraries, and techniques to remain at the forefront of your field.

Seek feedback. Don't hesitate to seek feedback on your work. Peer reviews, collaboration, and mentorship can lead to valuable insights and improvements.

9. Quality Assurance

Testing and validation. Develop unit tests for your code to ensure that changes do not introduce new errors. Automated testing frameworks can be a valuable asset in this regard.

10. Open Source Tools

Utilize open source tools. Open source software and libraries provide transparency and the ability to audit and modify code. Libraries like NumPy, pandas, and statsmodels for Python are widely used in econometric analysis.

These best practices serve as the foundation for robust econometric analysis. Following these principles not only improves the quality and reliability of your work but also

HAYDEN VAN DER POST

ensures that your findings are accessible and reproducible. By embracing these practices, you empower yourself to make impactful contributions to the field of econometrics and data science.

Debugging And Troubleshooting

Python is a powerful tool for econometric analysis, but like any tool, it may sometimes give you unexpected results or pose challenges. In this chapter, we'll explore debugging and troubleshooting techniques that will help you navigate through the intricacies of Python and econometric analysis. Think of this chapter as your toolkit for addressing common issues and ensuring your analysis runs smoothly.

1. Debugging with Precision

Debugging is akin to detective work, and precision matters. When an error arises in your code, the first step is to identify the source. Python offers several tools to pinpoint issues:

Print Statements: The simplest and often most effective debugging technique is using print statements. By strategically placing print statements in your code, you can check the values of variables and trace the flow of your program.

Debugger: Python comes with a built-in debugger module called pdb. You can set breakpoints, step through your code, and inspect variables interactively. Familiarizing yourself with this tool can save you hours of frustration.

Example:

python

```python
import pdb

def complex_calculation(x, y):
    result = x + y
    pdb.set_trace() # Set a breakpoint
    result *= 2
    return result

x = 5
y = 3
output = complex_calculation(x, y)
```

2. Handling Exceptions

Exception handling is a fundamental aspect of writing robust code. In econometrics, you often deal with complex data, and errors can occur. By handling exceptions gracefully, your analysis can continue running even if a part of it fails.

Try-Except Blocks: Use try and except blocks to capture and handle exceptions. This prevents the entire program from crashing if an error occurs.

Example:

python

```python
try:
```

```
    result = 10 / 0  # Division by zero
except ZeroDivisionError:
    result = None  # Handle the exception
```

3. Documentation and Comments

Effective documentation can often prevent the need for extensive debugging. By providing comments and docstrings, you make your code more understandable for yourself and others.

Docstrings: Use docstrings to describe the purpose and usage of functions and classes. This way, when you or others revisit the code, its functionality is clear.

Example:

python

```python
def calculate_average(values):
    """
    Calculate the average of a list of values.

    Args:
        values (list): List of numeric values.

    Returns:
        float: The calculated average.
    """
    total = sum(values)
```

```python
    return total / len(values)
```

4. Unit Testing

Unit tests are a developer's best friend. They allow you to verify that individual components of your code work correctly. Python provides several testing frameworks, such as unittest and pytest.

Example using unittest:

python

```python
import unittest

def square(x):
    return x * x

class TestSquareFunction(unittest.TestCase):
    def test_positive_numbers(self):
        self.assertEqual(square(5), 25)

    def test_negative_numbers(self):
        self.assertEqual(square(-3), 9)

if __name__ == '__main__':
    unittest.main()
```

5. Troubleshooting Common Errors

Understanding and addressing common errors can save you

time and frustration. Here are some of the most frequent Python issues you might encounter:

Indentation Errors: Python relies on indentation to define code blocks. Indentation errors can lead to syntax errors.

NameError: Occurs when a variable or function is used before it's defined.

TypeError: Happens when you use an object of the wrong data type.

SyntaxError: Indicates that there's a problem with the syntax of your code.

Example:

python

```
for i in range(5):
print(i) # IndentationError: expected an indented block
```

These are just a few of the strategies you can employ to debug and troubleshoot Python code effectively. The key is to approach troubleshooting with patience, systematic thinking, and the understanding that debugging is a natural part of the coding process.

Remember, even experienced programmers encounter errors. What sets them apart is their ability to diagnose and resolve issues efficiently. As you continue your journey in econometric analysis with Python, these debugging and troubleshooting skills will prove invaluable.

Staying Updated and Continuing Learning

As you've journeyed through this book, you've gained a strong foundation in Python for econometrics. You've explored essential concepts, practiced hands-on data analysis, and dived into various econometric techniques. But the world of data science and econometrics is a dynamic one, where new libraries, tools, and methodologies emerge regularly. In this section, we'll discuss strategies to keep your knowledge up-to-date and continue your learning journey.

1. Embrace Online Resources

The internet is a treasure trove of resources for Python and econometrics enthusiasts. Websites, forums, and online courses provide an abundance of information. Here's how to make the most of them:

Online Courses: Platforms like Coursera, edX, and Udemy offer courses that can deepen your understanding of both Python and econometrics. Look for courses that explore the latest trends and technologies.

Webinars and Workshops: Participate in webinars and workshops hosted by experts. They often discuss cutting-edge tools and applications. These interactive sessions can keep you informed about the latest advancements.

2. Python Communities and Forums

The Python community is vast and vibrant. Engaging with it can help you stay updated and address specific queries. Here's how you can leverage this resource:

Stack Overflow: A hub for developers, this Q&A platform can help you find solutions to Python issues. Engage with the community by both asking questions and providing answers.

Python Communities on Reddit: Subreddits like r/Python and r/learnpython are great for discussions on Python libraries, best practices, and news.

3. Blogs and Newsletters

Many data scientists and econometricians share their insights through blogs and newsletters. These platforms offer valuable articles, tutorials, and insights on the latest developments.

4. GitHub Repositories

GitHub is not just a platform for version control; it's also a repository for open-source Python projects. Explore GitHub to find libraries, tools, and projects that can enhance your Python skills.

5. Conferences and Seminars

Attend conferences and seminars related to data science, econometrics, and Python. These events provide an excellent opportunity to connect with experts and stay informed about the latest research and tools.

6. Python Libraries and Their Documentation

Python libraries are continually updated, and their documentation evolves. Make a habit of referring to the official documentation of libraries such as NumPy, pandas, and scikit-learn. You'll find updated features, improvements, and examples.

Example:

python

```
# Stay updated with the latest pandas library
import pandas as pd

# Check the latest version
latest_version = pd.__version__

# Read the release notes to see what's new
pandas_release_notes        =        pd.read_html('https://
pandas.pydata.org/docs/whatsnew/v' + latest_version + '.html')
```

7. Online Courses and Certifications

Enroll in advanced online courses and certifications that offer in-depth knowledge on specific Python libraries or econometric techniques. For example, you can explore machine learning courses, deep learning specializations, or econometrics certifications.

8. Practice with Real-world Projects

One of the best ways to learn and stay updated is by working on real-world projects. Challenge yourself with problems relevant to economics and econometrics, and apply the latest Python techniques to solve them.

A Journey of Continuous Learning

Staying updated in the dynamic world of Python and econometrics is not just a task but a journey. It's a journey that requires curiosity, engagement with the community, and the passion to learn. Python has proven to be a valuable tool in econometrics, and its evolution promises exciting developments.

With the strategies mentioned above, you can navigate this ever-changing landscape, ensuring that your Python skills and econometric knowledge remain at the cutting edge. As you continue your professional journey, remember that learning never stops, and each new piece of knowledge you acquire enriches your capabilities in econometric analysis. Keep exploring, keep learning, and keep growing.

In this book, we've strived to equip you with the knowledge and skills to excel in the field of econometrics using Python. Now, it's time to take the reins and continue your path of continuous learning. The world of Python in econometrics is full of opportunities, and you're well-prepared to seize them.

Conclusion and Key Takeaways

Congratulations on reaching the end of this comprehensive guide, "Python in Econometrics: Bridging Data Science and Economic Analysis." Throughout this book, you've embarked on a transformative journey, learning how Python can empower economists and data scientists to extract valuable insights from data and conduct in-depth econometric analyses. In this concluding chapter, we'll summarize the key takeaways from your remarkable expedition and explore the broader applications of Python in econometrics.

1. The Power of Python in Econometrics

Throughout the book, you've come to appreciate the immense potential of Python in the field of econometrics. Python's versatility, extensive libraries, and a thriving community make it a formidable tool for data analysis, modeling, and interpretation. Whether you're an aspiring economist, a seasoned data scientist, or someone in between, Python equips you with the means to tackle complex economic questions and generate meaningful answers.

2. The Python Environment

In Chapter 1, you were introduced to the world of Python and its relationship with econometrics. You explored the fundamentals of setting up your Python environment, mastering basic Python concepts, and venturing into econometric terminology. These building blocks have laid a solid foundation for your journey into the world of data analysis.

3. Data Preparation: The Crucial First Step

Chapter 2 Enlightened You On The Pivotal Role Of Data Preparation In Econometrics. You Acquired Knowledge About Data Types, Data Structures, Loading And Reading Data, Data Cleaning, Transformation, And Visualization. With These Skills, You're Now Capable Of Harnessing Raw Data To Uncover Patterns And Insights.

4. Basic Econometric Analysis

Chapters 3 and 4 delved into the heart of econometrics. You

gained a deep understanding of simple and multiple linear regression, time series analysis, and forecasting using ARIMA models. You also applied these techniques in a real-world context. The ability to employ regression models and forecast future trends is now at your fingertips.

5. Unpacking Panel Data

In Chapter 5, you ventured into the realm of panel data analysis. Here, you explored fixed and random effects models, endogeneity testing, and advanced panel data techniques. This advanced skill set allows you to address complex questions involving individual-level and time-series data.

6. Advanced Econometric Techniques

Chapter 6 Equipped You With The Knowledge Of Advanced Econometric Techniques, Including Instrumental Variable (Iv) Regression, Limited Dependent Variable Models, Cointegration, And Error Correction Models. These Techniques Empower You To Tackle Intricate Econometric Questions And Assess Policy Impacts Effectively.

7. The Machine Learning Revolution

Chapter 7 Unveiled The Fusion Of Machine Learning And Econometrics. You Discovered How To Utilize Supervised And Unsupervised Learning Techniques For Economic Prediction. As A Responsible Practitioner, You Explored Ethical Considerations In Machine Learning, Enhancing Your Decision-Making Skills.

8. Economic Modeling and Simulations

Chapter 8 provided insights into building economic models and conducting simulations. You learned to analyze simulation results and assess the impact of policy changes. This strategic knowledge enables you to make informed decisions in complex economic scenarios.

9. The Art of Data Visualization and Reporting

In Chapter 9, you honed the craft of data visualization. You discovered how to create advanced visualizations, interactive dashboards, and effective reports. These skills are essential for communicating your findings and policy recommendations to a broader audience.

10. Best Practices and Continuing Learning

Chapter 10 Guided You Through Best Practices In Coding, Analysis, And Documentation. You Also Learned About Debugging And Troubleshooting Common Issues. As The Final Section, You Explored Strategies For Staying Updated With The Latest Python Libraries And Continuing Your Learning Journey.

Beyond the Pages: The Broader Applications of Python in Econometrics

The applications of Python in econometrics extend far beyond the boundaries of this book. With Python in your toolbox, you're well-prepared to:

i. Contribute to Cutting-Edge Research: Python empowers you to conduct sophisticated econometric research and contribute to the advancement of economic theory and practice.

ii. Work in Academia and Research: With your newfound skills, you're equipped to pursue a career in academia, where you can teach and inspire the next generation of economists.

iii. Decision-Making in Public Policy: Your econometric expertise and Python skills make you an asset in public policy, where you can help design and evaluate impactful policies.

iv. Data-Driven Business Decisions: In the private sector, you can harness the power of Python and econometrics to drive data-driven decision-making, whether in finance, marketing, or management.

v. Entrepreneurship: For the entrepreneurial spirits, Python opens doors to innovative ventures in data analysis and econometric consulting.

The Unending Journey

The beauty of Python in econometrics lies in its continual evolution. New libraries and tools emerge, novel techniques are developed, and data science advances. Your journey in this field is not just a one-time exploration; it's a continuous learning process.

As you embark on your path beyond these pages, remember that the pursuit of knowledge is a lifelong endeavor. Stay curious, embrace new challenges, and stay engaged with the ever-expanding Python and econometrics community. Through each endeavor, you'll further cement your role as a proficient econometrician and data scientist.

"Python in Econometrics: Bridging Data Science and Economic Analysis" serves as a launchpad into the world of data-driven economic insights. You've honed your skills, acquired the tools, and embraced a mindset of continuous learning. With Python as your ally, you're well-equipped to navigate the intricate landscapes of economics and econometrics, extracting meaningful insights from data and driving impactful decisions. Your journey has just begun, and the possibilities are endless.

ADDITIONAL RESOURCES

Your journey through "Python in Econometrics: Bridging Data Science and Economic Analysis" has equipped you with a strong foundation in Python-based econometric analysis. However, the world of econometrics is vast and constantly evolving. To further enhance your knowledge and skills, it's essential to explore additional resources, including books, courses, websites, and communities dedicated to econometrics. This chapter presents a comprehensive list of valuable resources that will continue to guide you on your path to econometric excellence.

Books for In-Depth Learning:

"Econometric Analysis" by William H. Greene: This comprehensive book covers econometric theory and applications, making it an excellent resource for those seeking a deep understanding of econometrics.

"Time Series Analysis" by Jonathan D. Cryer and Kung-Sik Chan: For a focused exploration of time series analysis, this book provides the foundation you need to master this critical aspect of econometrics.

"Panel Data Econometrics" by Manuel Arellano: Dive into the world of panel data analysis with this text, which offers a rigorous treatment of the subject.

"Introduction to the Practice of Statistics" by David S. Moore, George P. McCabe, and Bruce A. Craig: This book provides an introduction to statistical concepts, which is essential for econometric analysis.

"Python for Data Analysis" by Wes McKinney: While not dedicated to econometrics, this book is invaluable for understanding data manipulation and analysis using Python, a skill crucial in econometrics.

Online Courses:

Coursera: Platforms like Coursera offer a wide range of econometrics courses, including options from prestigious institutions like the University of London and the University of California, Irvine.

edX: Explore econometrics courses on edX, including those from MIT and UC Berkeley, to gain insights from top educators.

Udemy: On Udemy, you can find practical courses that combine Python programming with econometric analysis.

Khan Academy: For beginners, Khan Academy offers a series of introductory videos on statistics and econometrics.

DataCamp: Sharpen your data analysis skills with DataCamp's courses in Python, data visualization, and statistics.

Websites and Online Resources:

Econometric Society (www.econometricsociety.org): The official website of the Econometric Society offers valuable publications and resources related to econometrics research.

The Econometrics Journal (onlinelibrary.wiley.com/journal/13689276): A peer-reviewed journal dedicated to econometrics, providing access to the latest research in the field.

Cross Validated (stats.stackexchange.com): A community-driven question and answer platform where you can find solutions to econometric problems and learn from fellow practitioners.

StatsModels (www.statsmodels.org): An open-source Python library for estimating and interpreting models for statistical and econometric analysis.

Econometrics by Simulation (econometricsbysimulation.com): This website offers interactive examples and simulations to aid in understanding econometric concepts.

Community and Forums:

Stack Overflow (stackoverflow.com): An excellent place to ask specific questions related to Python and econometrics and receive expert answers.

Reddit's r/econometrics (www.reddit.com/r/econometrics): Engage with a community of econometricians and data scientists, discussing trends, problems, and solutions.

LinkedIn Groups: Explore and join LinkedIn groups related to econometrics, data analysis, and Python programming to stay connected with professionals in the field.

Research and Journals:

Journal of Applied Econometrics: A leading journal in applied econometrics, which regularly publishes cutting-edge research and methodology.

The Review of Economic Studies (www.restud.com): This journal provides valuable insights into economic theory and econometric methods.

NBER (www.nber.org): The National Bureau of Economic Research offers a treasure trove of working papers and research publications on various economic topics.

IDEAS (ideas.repec.org): An online resource that provides access to economic research, including working papers, articles, and software.

Econometrics Software:

R (www.r-project.org): If you want to explore econometrics using R, this open-source language and environment for statistical computing is a powerful tool.

STATA (www.stata.com): STATA is widely used in econometric analysis and offers a suite of features for data manipulation and modeling.

EViews (www.eviews.com): A specialized software package for time series and cross-sectional data analysis, commonly used in econometrics.

Econometric Organizations:

The American Economic Association (www.aeaweb.org): This association provides valuable resources for economists and econometricians, including journals, data, and events.

International Association for Applied Econometrics (www.iaae.org): An organization dedicated to promoting the use of econometrics and its applications.

Your journey through econometrics and Python is a continuous learning process. By exploring these additional resources, you can expand your knowledge, stay updated with the latest developments, and connect with a community of fellow econometricians. Whether you aspire to excel in academia, contribute to groundbreaking research, or drive data-driven decisions in the business world, these resources will serve as your guiding light on this intellectually stimulating path. As you delve deeper into econometrics, remember that the pursuit of knowledge is a never-ending voyage, and your passion and curiosity will be your greatest allies.

Printed in Great Britain
by Amazon

36968065R10130